# DARE

## to Be

# Happier

D0550188

To Vicky
And one day, she
decided to be happier
~ is your new story.
Dare to be happier,
Caroline XXX

This edition published in 2019 by
Eddison Books Limited
www.eddisonbooks.com

Text copyright © Caroline Johnstone 2019
Design copyright © Eddison Books Limited 2019
Cover design by Abi Read

The right of Caroline Johnstone to be identified as the author of this
work has been asserted by her in accordance with the Copyright,
Designs and Patents Act 1988.

All rights reserved. No part of this book may be reproduced,
stored in a retrieval system, or transmitted in any form or by any
means without the prior written permission of the publisher, nor be
otherwise circulated in any form of binding or cover other than that
in which it is published and without a similar condition including this
condition being imposed on the subsequent purchaser.

British Library Cataloguing-in-Publication data available on request.

ISBN 978-1-85906-448-1

1 3 5 7 9 10 8 6 4 2

Printed in Europe


Eddison Books Limited

Managing Director **Lisa Dyer**
Managing Editor **Nicolette Kaponis**
Copy Editor **Katie Hewett**
Proofreader **Jane Donovan**
Indexer **Stephen Blake**
Designer **Penny Stock**
Production **Sarah Rooney**

# DARE

## to Be
## Happier

Live your best life
through 25 journalling lessons

Caroline Johnstone

Eddison Books Ltd

# Contents

# Introduction

## OUR INNER VOICE SILENCED

Most of us are stressed, overwhelmed and exhausted – too busy getting through each day to have anything more than a fleeting idea of who we really want to be, or what we want to do or have in our lives. We may be successful but we have no time to enjoy our lives, or we may feel that we are a failure and there is no point in trying to do things differently. Either way, we certainly aren't living our lives consciously or with intent. If we are being honest, we keep ourselves busy for good reasons; we are often too afraid to ask ourselves the questions we know we should be asking, in case we realize how much of our lives we are wasting on things and people that don't really matter to us. And then we wonder why we feel so depressed, stuck and purposeless.

People as varied as Maya Angelou, C. S. Lewis, Albert Einstein, Nelson Mandela, Fergie from The Black Eyed Peas and Oprah Winfrey swear that they have intentionally created their best lives by using a simple tool: journalling. They know from experience what the experts are increasingly proving scientifically – journalling works to improve your mental and physical health.

'Since the mid-1980s an increasing number of studies have focused on the value of expressive writing as a way to bring about healing. The evidence is mounting that the act of writing about traumatic experience for as little as 15 or 20 minutes a day for three or four days can produce measurable changes in physical and mental health. Emotional writing can also affect people's sleep habits, work efficiency, and how they connect with others.'

James W. Pennebaker, internationally-renowned social psychologist

## LIVE YOUR BEST LIFE, INTENTIONALLY

As someone who has been journalling for many years and who runs countless workshops, I know the amazing results journalling can bring. It creates a space for you to slow down your life and reflect on it; it allows you to silence the outside world and listen to the richness of your inner world; and it also supports you in making the changes that mean you are intentionally living your best life. Finally!

When was the last time you deliberately slowed down enough to give yourself the space to think, breathe, listen to your heart and to see if the life you are living is the life that you really want?

Occasionally, we may be given the opportunity to think about how we are living our lives when a holiday or an illness means we are unable to carry out our normal routine. Sometimes, the universe has to grab us by the shoulders and force us to see what is happening, and as I get older I'm finding this is the hard way to learn I need to change. Now, I make conscious decisions to stop and reflect on my life. I make an appointment with myself most mornings to do this because I know if I wait until later, there will usually be something more 'important' or 'urgent' to do, and if that is the case, I rarely manage to find the time. I also set aside time in my diary for myself each week for longer periods of reflection, or as I'm heading towards a crisis point of some sort, because I know it is critical to allow myself that time to make better decisions. I simply write 'keep free' in my diary, and unless it's an emergency, I just say I am not available as I'm already busy. I am: I'm investing in me.

Let's not kid ourselves; our busy-ness serves a purpose unless we examine it further. It prevents us from looking at ourselves in the mirror. It stops us from listening to our incessant thoughts, and from dealing with what is causing our less than totally comfortable feelings. This means it is harder to quieten that inner critic that reminds us (untruthfully) how unworthy we are when it tries to stop us from failing. Our refusal to reflect on our lives means we don't confront our insecurities, or face what needs to be faced; we can numb ourselves and stay within our comfort zone.

And then we wonder why we feel so exhausted, why we have no more to give to those around us, why all we do is beat a retreat at every chance we can, or exist by living a half-life, or find ourselves living out someone else's plans for our lives. What if you learned instead to be real, to trust what you are feeling inside no matter what anyone outside is telling you, if you started to say no to others and say yes to yourself? What if you were able to reconnect with what really matters, start reshaping your life so you are calmer, more at peace, mindful, happier? Don't you deserve that? You can't keep running on empty. Journalling is a tool you will find to be your refuge and retreat, as well as a joy, a change agent, a blessing, a catalyst, a confidante.

## MY HAVEN

Journalling is certainly my haven. It is in this silence and space that I find I can go from anxiety, fear and the feeling of being overwhelmed back to happiness, peace and balance. There are so many different journalling tools you can use; your journal can be as colourful and creative as you like – or it can just be words – as long as it expresses whatever it is your soul needs to say and empowers you to follow through.

I've been journalling since I was a child. For a while, as an adult I forgot to do it, but I started again in earnest in 2002. In 2006, when I was depressed and stressed (mainly because I wasn't listening to my inner wisdom), I learned the value of a gratitude journal. Since then, gratitude is an almost daily part of my life. I choose to use a journal most days; you may choose to use it less – there's no hard and fast rule. There are, after all, only a few rules about journalling. Ultimately though, how and when you journal is about how it fits with you as a practice to help you grow; you just need to do it regularly, do it honestly, and start listening to what your emotions are telling you.

When journalling, there is no point just writing in at a surface level, simply recording events (as in a diary), or skirting around how you are feeling or what you think. You must commit to being totally honest with yourself for it to be effective. Once you make that commitment, you'll discover the power of journalling.

## A SAFE PLACE

As you begin to write out your thoughts, feelings and emotions, you will find your journal is a safe place that allows you to do this. You start to express more, including what you had previously kept trapped inside through fear. Then you begin to see patterns of behaviour or beliefs that are less than totally useful; you will see signposts that were there all along but you were going too fast to see them. You will realize that it's OK to start to question your own thinking, as not all of it is true. You step into a world where you come to terms with who you are and accept and approve of yourself (knowing you have only ever done the best you could with what you had), and you will find that you become your own alchemist. You learn to turn less than totally positive experiences into the gold of spiritual change. You will recognize that you are your own guru, teacher, healer, coach, best friend.

## YOUR OWN DEEP INNER WISDOM

If you're like me, you simply need reminders that your happiness lies in your own hands, that you can get too comfortable within your own comfort zone, and that it takes courage to change what needs to be changed – but you can do things when you are scared. If you have ever been unhappy, confused, stuck, overwhelmed, exhausted, run from your feelings, not done what you know you should have done, not set the boundaries needed to protect your values, then you have simply forgotten to access your inner wisdom or listen to it.

## AN ALL-IN-ONE TOOLBOX

When you journal, as well as everything else mentioned in the previous section, it helps you accept responsibility for change by seeing who you might be blaming from your past or present. It helps you develop a growth mindset where you are willing to try, rather than have a fixed mindset that means you stay where you are, trying to control the outside world and other people. It is a fantastic tool to get you out of your comfort zones – where the power lies.

It's a way of developing the habit of gratitude – the number one thing that will change your life. This is a place to record what you are grateful for, which means you start looking for more things to add to your list. As your focus changes, your attitude shifts, and as your thinking starts to change, what you feel will change – and then what you do will change: *it has to*. It is a personal development tool that allows you to observe your life and learn about yourself, identifying patterns or habits that repeat themselves, or in dealing with emotions and feelings that you try to numb when they keep calling for attention. It will help you build your own inner strength and resilience – that ability to bounce back from difficult times, to cope with major changes or crises, or reframe them in a way that moves you forwards rather than living in the past.

## STILL NEED A REASON TO START?

There's no good reason for you not to dive in and start – but if you need a reason, start at the beginning of this book and work your way through each chapter. Or, you can look through the contents and read the chapters that resonate with you now. I don't accept that you are too busy to invest this time in yourself. As I have said before, 'If you don't have time to invest 15 or 20 minutes in yourself, then you are too busy.' In this book, I've provided themed guided questions on each of the reasons (or steps) to journal. You will be able to answer some of them easily, some will need more thought, and others you won't want to answer. Don't avoid the hard questions. Sit with those questions and allow yourself to answer them; let go and be free, moving forwards instead of holding pain firmly and causing it to crystallize.

It is never too late to embrace a new way of life. Creating a happier future starts by how you live now; that's where your reality begins and ends. Happiness is in your hands – stop giving it to other people to control and start living consciously. Come, let's start the adventure of living our best lives.

P.S. Do feel free to share your learnings with me at caroline@daretobehappier.com. I'd love to hear from you.

# 1 Be your own alchemist

'You are an alchemist;
make gold of that.'
*William Shakespeare*

## The universal elixir

Alchemy is the process of transformation, an almost magical process of change. If you look at journalling in that light, you will certainly be your own alchemist, as you can use it to transform your whole life and create new things and new ways of being.

## Transform your life

At the outset, you may not believe this is possible. You may feel stuck, or you might have tried and failed many times to change, or the change you want seems like a mountain you can't possibly climb. I know that we are all capable of this transformation, to develop different ways of seeing and being, and to overcome obstacles (including our patterns of failure), if we want to. Too often, we live a life that is not the one we want but one we've settled into as it feels comfortable – the easy familiarity that is the lifestyle, job, relationships and beliefs we have (even when these were not ours in the first place or no longer suit us). And yet we wonder why we feel unhappy, why we fill our need for 'more' with material goods as a way to satiate our restless discontent. Our soul will keep calling until we listen – regardless of the excuses we use not to grow (such as our personality, background or the expectations of our family or the community around us). We cling to the past and live under the constraints of the caterpillar when we could fly free like a butterfly.

## HOLDING ON TO THE FAMILIAR

We like our comfort zones and fear transformation because it is the unknown. Who might we become? Who might we leave behind? What might change ask of us? Can we handle the change – or the hurdles or pushbacks? Who are we to shine, anyway? Yet through our fear, we need to notice that we are often prodded (by our unhappiness, depression and anxiety that remind us to change, or by small, seemingly insignificant events or seismic changes to our circumstances) to be all that we can be, to stop standing in our light and shine as we long to shine. Unlike the alchemists of old, who failed and tried again and again in their constant search – knowing the search was worth the failures that taught them something – we hold ourselves back from trying new things. What you've been doing so far hasn't worked so it's time to act as an alchemist by taking small steps to change, knowing we can leave any experience behind us and learn lessons from it that will still move us forwards.

Does that feel like too much effort, like it can't be done, especially by you? Then your focus is wrong; you are focusing on yourself and not what you want. The alchemists knew the size of their task, to find the elixir to eternal life, for many said it was an impossible task. That didn't deter them; they focused on what they wanted, not on any perceived lack of reality, resources or their own capabilities. They knew that our hearts will not fail us when we determine to live life consciously, for our highest good, because that is how we honour our time here and that is how we contribute to the world.

## THE ART OF FOCUS

The alchemy in journalling occurs because of such focus. You probably already know the area of your life that most needs attention, so why not begin by deciding to focus on that? Here's how it worked for me. After a particularly intense time in my life, I realized I needed to take time out to look after me. I gave myself a year to re-read Louise Hay's book, *You Can Heal Your Life*, and also decided to have a concentrated period to focus on nurturing myself. I have blogged about parts of that journey, what I called Project Me 101 (*see page 208*). I gathered a team of friends, life coaches and anam caras (deep soul friends) around me for support. Team Caroline was there to keep me accountable to take action on what I discovered or decided. Unusually for me, I started by making small changes – not pushing myself in exercising so I injured myself, taking time to read a book rather than scrolling through my phone, having coffee instead of lunch with a friend (when I don't enjoy the lunch as I am concentrating on the conversation not the food).

## TEAM CAROLINE

I met a member of Team Caroline and her first words were, 'When are you going to stop being so hard on yourself?' It was a good question. And the answer was NOW – that was the idea of this project. She probed further: 'What does it mean to you to nurture yourself?' I replied, 'It means looking after me first. It means being gentle on myself, and it means slowing down and finding balance.' 'Yes,' she said, 'but HOW?'

'I'm going to nurture my body by choosing a healthier diet; I'm going to get outside more, walk and cycle more; I'm going to have massages; I'm going to read again just for the sheer fun of it. And I'm going to learn to stop multitasking.' 'But you're a woman,' she said, 'it's what we do.'

I understood that, but I had been reading new research on multitasking and how it means you're not really present in whatever you are doing, and how it often means you don't do any one thing well. But – and it's a big but – I couldn't give her any more examples of how I might nurture myself. I ended up researching 'how to nurture you'. I found many examples of 'how to nurture your child', or 'how to nurture your nurture' – but it wasn't nearly as easy to find ideas about how to nurture me. So I decided to at least start journalling about nurturing my inner child and my creativity, as a means to understanding what nurtured my body, mind and spirit. I found it doesn't matter where you start, it matters that you start.

Another member of Team Caroline, Jane Talbot, gave me a great list of questions to journal (see page 208), but I resisted answering them. Then came day three. I was stuck, everything seemed too hard. I had more questions than answers – and I had moved my focus back to how I was living instead of how I wanted to live. So I had a pity party, where I didn't feel like journalling about anything.

Day four arrived and I was in a different mood. I found that my decision to nurture myself was being supported by those around me and, in the way that decisions often spread, it started to change others too. A member of Team Caroline changed phones to give herself a break from social media as a way of nurturing herself.

I started to accept that I was learning a new way of being, relaxing my need to organize everything with military precision. I started to check in with myself as part of living more consciously by asking these two questions that someone else suggested: What am I feeling right now? What do I need?

## DON'T EXPECT CHANGE TO BE AN EASY RIDE

When you start to live more consciously, life doesn't automatically get easier. It often gets harder. By day five, changes were coming so fast it was hard to catch my breath and I forgot my decision to live consciously and went on autopilot. When I reflected on this in my journal, I said that I felt that it was as if by looking after myself, I had taken my eyes off everyone else. I wasn't in a great mood; I felt really stuck, like this was all a pointless exercise.

I then remembered I was on a journey of significance for the spirit and the heart to find out how to better care for myself. I started to journal the answers to Jane's questions. I realized I knew what nurturing meant and I knew how to do it. It meant being grateful, nurturing myself with good food and the sleep I needed. It meant time spent with dear friends. I saw that nourishment is the dance of balancing body, mind and spirit.

## TIME FOR YOU TO BE AN ALCHEMIST

You already know the area of your life that needs attention most. It could be your relationships, career, time management, creativity or something completely different. When you start to journal freely about it (using different tools and questions), you will find that paying attention to it changes things *and* starts to change all other areas of your life. You will begin to understand, or be reminded, that you should lead your life in a way that corresponds with your values, live your dream and control your destiny. You learn that when you truly want something, and when that desire aligns with who you are and your purpose, then the universe takes your hand and together you watch miracles unfold. If that's not magic, I don't know what is.

# Be your own alchemist

**1** What old identities, roles or labels would it be helpful to let go of?

**2** What are you excited about at this point in your life?

**3** What lessons from the past are helping you now?

**4** What do you need to do today to create the future you dream of?

**5** What changes might you be resisting, and why?

**6** What might be different because of these changes?

**7** What will you lose?

**8** What might you gain?

**9** What do you need to let go of?

**10** Can you pay the price the changes might demand of you?

## Choose a thought to concentrate on from the choices below:

I change the world just by being in it and I can change it by what I create for it.

I am transforming into all I should be and all that I already am.

# Learn the magic of choice

'In the long run, we
shape our lives, and we
shape ourselves. The process
never ends until we die. And
the choices we make are
ultimately our responsibility.'

*Eleanor Roosevelt*

**It's easier to make choices from silence than chaos**

We live in an overwhelming world that is full of noise, chaos and confusion. What we need is a clear head and silence to be able to pause and think deeply, listening to what our heart and intuition are saying. Hindsight then teaches us where we should have considered things more carefully or listened to our intuition. Journalling is powerful, but not simple, as you need to make a commitment to put in the time and effort.

Once you start writing, you will see that even where you felt stuck you *can* create options, or you can narrow down choices, or see the big picture where previously you were focusing only on one or two points. You might begin to get a feel for what was really niggling you about the issue in the first place. There is a wide variety of tools you can use to help you 'think' your way through issues to come up with solutions as you sort through problems; or help you see what you need to give attention to, throw out, deal with now or at a later point. Three of the best are stream of consciousness writing (letting your thoughts flow and writing down everything that comes to mind), clustering (*see page 133*) and lists of one hundred, in which you write down your issue or question on a piece of paper and come up with one hundred solutions. Your subconscious mind will naturally engage in the process and surprising answers will reveal themselves.

By using these tools, you can determine what really matters to you, stop going round in circles and allow your own wisdom to come to the surface. Consequently you will make wiser choices where there is no conflict with your values, as you've listened to your heart.

## BEHAVIOUR CHANGES WHEN YOU WATCH IT

You can change anything you want to when you pay attention to it, question it and take action. The Hawthorne Effect is the name for the theory that says behaviour changes when it is being observed. If you think that is true, then we must learn to watch our own behaviour. Transfer your thinking onto paper and see what you really have to face, as once you can see it, you will be able to organize it, review it and discard it. Find the answers.

## CHOICES WHEN LIFE'S CIRCUMSTANCES ARE HARD

Even when we follow our heart's desire and know we are in the flow of life, sometimes things can be less than positive. Illness, redundancy and loss of loved ones are all part of our existence.

Some of these things we may bring on ourselves, but others will be outside our control; our soul learns its lessons from both. Some would say that at a soul level, we choose all our experiences. Whatever your beliefs are – and mine are that I am open to learning what my soul needs to learn and I'd prefer to do that easily rather than through pain – we need a way of dealing with any experience so we don't get stuck in the past, continuing to hold onto things that no longer serve us well. The stories we keep telling ourselves about what has happened or is happening are often where we are a victim or searching for sympathy or validation. There comes a time when we need to choose a better story to create our future from and when to let the experience go (while learning the lessons). We can then gently allow ourselves to own our power and find the strength and wisdom to move towards a better life.

The experience itself is not what matters. What floors you could be a pebble in someone else's shoe. When I worked as a secretary as part of a mental health team, but was looking at where my career might go, I considered training as a psychologist. I had long conversations with the psychiatrists and psychologists who visited the centre, trying to see if they could explain why two people with very similar backgrounds and experiences could go on to live in such different ways. As they struggled to answer, I realized that it must be something more than the experience itself; it must be how the individuals involved processed that experience. It must be connected to who a person is, what had happened to them before, and how they thought about it and themselves.

## HOW WE CREATE OUR REALITY

After I chose not to study this area (instead focusing on Human Resource Management, which led me to Neuro-linguistic Programming or NLP), I found that the NLP Communication Model helped me understand these differences. It shows that we create our own reality in the way we filter experience through our values, beliefs, memories and previous experiences, and even how we prefer to think as we choose to delete or distort information, or generalize it, all of which depends on our emotional states. Ultimately, what happens in my life and what I choose to let that do to me or where it leads me is determined by how I process it. The buck stops with me, which is what William James, sometimes called the Father of American Psychology, meant when he said, 'The greatest discovery of my generation is that a human being can alter his life by altering his attitudes.'

Starting with what James taught about happiness and choices led me on a great journey of discovery. I now know that to understand that we are ultimately responsible for our lives and how we respond to what happens to us in any given set of circumstances is a powerful, life-changing concept. Your attitudes, feelings, thoughts and emotions are not fixed, your life is not fixed. You can change any of them; you just need to become aware of them.

When things are less than positive, your brain can freeze so you can only see the problem. In your journal, brainstorm an issue and come up with options where previously you saw none. Take an experience and start writing out your memories, feelings, thoughts and beliefs about it. Once you have these written down, you can start to change any one of them. You can change the memories as you can choose to see the circumstance from different perspectives or to change the focus of your story. You are in control of your own happiness, and of what happens next.

## YOUR CHOICES MAKE UP YOUR LIFE

Life happens. You can always learn something from it, such as how to make better choices, set better boundaries, stand up for yourself sooner, say yes or no, or stop. It's what you think, do and feel that makes you who you are. Journalling helps me see any experience in a different way, a way that supports rather than dampens my spirit. I have learned to trust my unconscious mind to be open to the wisdom inside and take the next step. Sometimes that may lead me to end or change relationships, sometimes it may lead me to counselling or other forms of therapy, sometimes it may take me to a place where I forgive the past and let it go, or just be gentle on myself.

In 2003, Denis Gallant and Robert Lafrenière wrote about their research into journalling as a tool for those who had lived with alcoholic parents. They wanted to see if it could help them process that experience and concluded it did help, even where people had blocked the experiences from their mind. We block parts of our history as a way of protecting ourselves and then firmly believe that they are no longer an issue for us because we've 'dealt with them', when in fact our life often demonstrates the opposite. If the experience was deeply traumatic, it is best to seek professional help to support you through changing things for the better; otherwise, honest journalling helps you process most other experiences.

There's a good chance you will, at some point, be faced with significant challenges. These might overwhelm you for a while, but you will find your centre again if you allow yourself, through friends, books and external wisdom, and the inner wisdom and strength you discover through your journals.

When choices need to be made, you can go with the flow and let them overwhelm you. Or, by using your journal to explore all of what is happening, as well as your thoughts and feelings, you can start to take back control. You decide what to learn from the experience, what to change, how to be more resourceful or curious. You have the power of choice – learn to make those choices that support your happiness, to live your best life.

# Learn the magic of choice

1 What options do you have? If you can't see options, who do you know who is good at generating them?

2 Are you clear about the ultimate choice you need or want to make?

3 Do you have sufficient information to make the best choice you can? What other information might you need?

**4** Can you narrow the number of options down to two choices (and then do a list of positive and negative points, or write down words associated with each one)?

**5** Which choice sits best with your values and overall purpose?

**6** What fears do you have about a choice you are facing? How many are real?

**7** What is the worst thing that could happen if you make the wrong choice?

**8** What advice would you give your best friend in similar circumstances now?

**9** If you are making a choice, whose voice do you hear telling you which one you should take?

**10** Put your hand on your stomach or heart: which of your choices feels better?

## Choose a thought to concentrate on from the choices below:

There is no failure, only feedback. I make a decision and then learn from it and move on.

I trust myself to learn how to make the best decisions for me and those I love.

'One's suffering disappears
when one lets oneself
go, when one yields –
even to sadness.'

*Antoine de Saint-Exupéry*

# 3 Get the emotions out

### A listening ear

There are times when we all need someone to listen to us, particularly when strong emotions or feelings are involved (unless we choose not to acknowledge them and numb or stifle them instead). Friends and family will often support us through these times, although sometimes we need to remember to reach out and ask for (and receive) the help available.

The good news is that you don't need to turn to a person every time you really need to talk, or process information or feelings. Much of the time, you are perfectly capable of doing that yourself via your journal, and once you have tried it a few times you realize that you often have the answers to resolve or calm things yourself and you learn how resilient you can be.

### A safe place to vent

When it comes to venting emotions (where you let them out but are not necessarily making any sense of them as you do so), your journal is often an even better option than talking to someone else, particularly if what you are saying could affect their relationship with another person (in terms of how they view them).

I remember my dad telling me that if I was going to argue with my husband then it was best done without witnesses, as in most instances we would have forgotten what the argument was about long before the person hearing it did.

He wasn't saying don't get heated, don't let your emotions be seen or expressed; he was saying it's important to let those emotions out, but to choose how and when you do that. It's never helpful to block or ignore how we are feeling, repress those feelings or tell yourself and others that you are 'fine'. 'I'm fine' is probably the biggest lie in the world that we tell anyone (and one that no one believes anyway). A failure to express our emotions ultimately leads to addiction (as we develop a pattern of numbing), depression and/or health issues (including those affecting the heart). It simply isn't a healthy coping mechanism and it affects the rest of our lives, because when we dampen down emotions rather than feeling them, this means we do that to both healthy and unhealthy emotions.

Putting our thoughts down on paper transforms their ability to affect us. Even though it may be painful to do so, it forces us to acknowledge how we feel and name our emotions rather than saying we don't know what the matter is. In this way we can be angry and say we are angry, why that might be and how it is affecting us.

## LEARNING TO RECOGNIZE OUR EMOTIONS

By naming emotions, we start to identify those that are unhealthy, such as resentment, shame or high levels of anger or fear, and start to deal with the root causes or the thinking that creates them. For instance, anger never comes out of the blue; it is preceded by our thinking about what has happened, even if that thinking and reaction takes place in a split second. Since it is this process that matters for this chapter, focus on expressing the feeling, rather than the words themselves, in a safe space. If you can't get to your journal but still need to 'talk', then find some paper and just start writing. It is this immediacy, the ability to process your experience as it happens, that is important, so that what could have become a forest fire often becomes a flash in the pan. You deal with it and you move on, instead of being overwhelmed by the emotion, affected more deeply as it escalates quickly or sabotaged in the future by driving it underground. Also, you may even find the trigger event was never that important, or you are able to capture what you needed so you can recognize the real problems or issues. Then at least you can develop a strategy for what happens next. What's not powerful about you releasing what's not serving you to create the space and energy for the rest of your life?

# Get the emotions out

Write out your emotions by doing any of these exercises using stream of consciousness writing (*see page 20*) or clustering (*see page 133*); use a separate piece of paper you can destroy if need be:

Name your emotion. Think of how you are feeling as if it were a shape, colour or song. Change the shape, the size of the shape, the colour or intensity of the colour, the type of music and write about how that makes you feel. Imagine your life now is a movie. What would you like the ending to be?

In the context of the emotion you are feeling, write down why you are feeling the way you are. What triggered this? What value or belief did you feel was attacked? How was this emotion dealt with as you grew up? Is it OK for you to express this emotion?

## Write about:

**1** How easy do you find explaining your emotions?

**2** Which emotion is it time to release?

**3** Which emotions do you regularly avoid? Why might that be?

**4** Do you label emotions in a negative way – perhaps anger as 'bad'? Is there a 'good' type of anger? How do you label other emotions?

**5** What is the main feeling with which you associate when thinking of a particular person or situation?

**6** What is this emotion trying to tell you?

## Choose a thought to concentrate on from the choices below:

'Let's not forget that the little emotions are the great captains of our lives.' *Van Gough*

I give myself permission to meet my own emotional needs.

# 4 **Find balance**

'Happiness is not a
matter of intensity
but of balance, order,
rhythm and harmony.'
*Thomas Merton*

### When our lives control us, we're out of balance

Every day we are given twenty-four hours or 1,440 minutes. How we use our time is how we create our life. If we don't control it consciously, it will end up controlling us — and then our life becomes everything we do not want it to be. Our existence is dominated by a hamster wheel of everything we believe we need to live in the way we have decided to.

Too often, it is not so much a hamster wheel as a rat trap. Sooner or later, we find we are stressed about the demands placed on our time and energy, never stopping to think if that time is being spent on things we don't really value, or people we don't really like or want to spend time with. We live in a world where time seems to keep going faster and where we keep getting busier. We watch our lives unfold as bystanders, we are exhausted and feel we can no longer cope.

## FIGURE OUT WHAT YOU ARE DOING AND WHY

We've forgotten that it is usually up to us how we apportion the hours and minutes we have at our disposal. Occasionally, external circumstances will lead to additional duties and responsibilities on top of our overflowing lists, perhaps when we need to unexpectedly provide care for someone. At such times, we absolutely must review everything we are doing to proritize what needs to happen first. However, most of the time we aren't faced with a dilemma like this – we simply haven't stopped to evaluate our lives to determine why we are doing what we are doing and whether or not it still fits with our values and who we are now. One of the best choices you will make is to prioritize your own life, by investing in yourself and journalling.

## CREATE THE TIME YOU NEED FOR YOU

Perhaps you can't imagine carving any time out for yourself to do this because your life is out of control. You know it, but you do not have the energy to deal with it and stress hormones like adrenalin and cortisol have kicked in so you don't digest your food so well or sleep soundly enough to recover. You have enough to do just to get through everything you need to do each day without trying to fit in relaxation or fun. You can either take time out to resolve things, or your body and mind will do that for you and enforce the time to change – through illness. At this stage, some people collapse and others literally run away and disappear from the madness of their current life forever. Don't do that.

## COMMIT TO CHANGE

Instead of running away, commit to changing for the better. Decide to protect your physical and emotional safety and make the necessary changes to both your external *and* internal environment. You can't just talk yourself out of stress by saying you will cope with it, 'have to cope with it', or you will cope 'until' a particular point or project or matter comes to an end. Our thinking processes are vital to stress (and how we handle it) as well as to change. It is not enough to try to stop thinking certain thoughts; we find this hard enough to do at the best of times and our ability to do so is greatly reduced when we are stressed. Dr Dan Wagner of Harvard University calls this an 'ironic process', where we actually achieve the opposite of what we wanted – resulting in an increase in our level of stress.

This inability to control our minds with our minds means that some people will try anything to shut them off or distract them by relying on alcohol or drugs. Taking deep breaths will calm us down a little, as will the practice of mindfulness, but we must create the space to deal with our lives and the thoughts, beliefs and attitudes that have created the stress in the first place.

## FIGURE OUT THE PROBLEM

When life is out of control you need to understand why this might be. Any sort of self-care can be a Herculean task, but it's worth every ounce of effort. By taking time out for yourself, you begin to see the patterns of behaviour that have led to where you are; you start to remember your values, you listen again to your own heart, spirit and dreams. You can use tools like the Eisenhower Matrix, which Stephen Covey's time management matrix went on to develop further, to help determine the difference between the urgent and the important. President Eisenhower said, 'What is important is seldom urgent and what is urgent is seldom important.' Important tasks usually require consideration and planning to ensure they happen; urgent tasks can stop us focusing on what is important because we have to react to what is happening. Spending time planning is not wasted, and knowing what is important means that you spend less time getting caught up in things that don't really matter.

Then you can use your journal to work on the beliefs and values that have led to this point: for instance, do you feel what you do must be perfect? Do you have to be a success? Do you need to stay in a job you hate? Do you have to have those holidays or clothes or gadgets? Do you need to maintain your own or your child's social life? Do you have to do it all yourself? Do you always have to say yes? When you have answered these questions you can start to implement plans to support the changes you need to make in order to live in accordance with your values.

Journalling helps bring us to a place where our mind is stilled, where we can see the wisdom of our own heart and gain the strength to go on to the next thing that we feel we must do or continue after evaluation or see what we must change. Creating the space to journal in such times – and then making it a core part of your life – means that your life will calm down as you see what you need to really want or need to prioritize or do. We give ourselves the chance to focus on our own priorities and realize the power in saying yes to what we really want to do or be, or have in our lives.

## INVEST IN YOUR LIFE

Journalling really shows its power here. It allows you to take time out of a busy life to ask yourself the questions you need to ask regarding your soul's purpose, as well as allowing you to examine the way you live now for clues about how you need to change things. It helps you realize what is or isn't working in your life. Often it helps you see that a reason to work in a particular job isn't the same thing as purpose.

The changes can be as rapid or as gradual as you want. You will have the freedom to dream bigger and then create goals and resolutions to support you in achieving them, breaking down larger tasks into the smaller ones needed to complete a project, which will help calm you down when under pressure. You will learn to invest time in yourself so you no longer waste time and energy on things that add no value to your life. If you find you need to work on your assertion skills, or set new or firmer boundaries to protect yourself, you will find reasons – and tools, such as a wheel of life – to do so.

A wheel of life is a great visual way to picture how you spend your time. I did a basic wheel of life, divided into eight segments, with the headings of career, family, leisure, spirituality, wellbeing, friends, fun/social life and money. I then, using a scale of 1–10, estimated how satisfied I was with the time I actually spent in each area. I realized that working, commuting and housework left little time for anything else, but it was a starting point. I consciously designed how I wanted my life to be and created headings that mattered (like joyful work, connecting, family, friends, writing, adventures, wellbeing and spirituality). This kept me focused on what I really valued. Try it. Once you've done the assessment of your current wheel of life, create headings you want to build a life you want. Even if you decide to change nothing, the good news is that the simple act of writing about the emotions and feelings underlying the lack of balance in your life is often enough to reduce the mental distress around it.[1-4]

# Find balance

To find balance, keep an activity log for two to three weeks.
This will help you see what you really do in a typical week. Then
answer these questions:

1 What takes up the bulk of your time?

2 What can you change about that?

3 Where do you waste time unnecessarily?

4 What are you doing that others could be doing?

**5** What could you do to help you keep on top of things?

**6** What could stop you keeping on top of things?

## In the context of living a balanced life, provide ten answers for each statement:

I want …

I am overwhelmed by …

I need to urgently deal with …

I will not …


I need to ask for …


I feel deprived of ….


I am willing …


## Choose a thought to concentrate on from the choices below:

Today, I make choices that result in my life having a good balance of what matters to me.

When I need to, I know I can say no, I can ask for help or I can take a short break.

# 5 Transform your professional life

'The will to win, the desire to succeed, the urge to reach your full potential ... these are the keys that will unlock the door to personal excellence.'

*Confucius*

## Why a work journal ... works!

There have been a number of scientific studies on the use of journals at work and the results show it benefits managers and employees, particularly if they wish to improve in their role or job. A journal is particularly helpful when used as a reflective tool to observe our own behaviour and actions because of the insight or feedback gained about patterns or behaviours as well as gaps in knowledge or training. It can also be used for goal-setting, for working on relationships, for helping you decide how you will develop yourself or other and it can also be used to brainstorm ideas if you use a tool such as mind-mapping or clustering (*see page 133*). It helps you get from where you are now to where you want to be by enabling you to be clear on your outcomes and then to persevere and stay focused when you need to.

## Building emotional intelligence through reflection

Emotional intelligence – the ability to understand and manage your emotions – is now considered by many to be more important for success than your IQ. Though some people are born with higher levels of emotional intelligence, it is something that can be learned and taught, and journalling will be a key tool in helping you develop and improve yours. Use it to reflect on your actions, consider how you felt about a particular situation or how others reacted. There is no failure, only feedback, so you use the information gained to help make changes and improvements.

It is the act of reflection that is the difference that makes the difference. Plato argued that 'all learning has an emotional base', and many researchers have taken this ancient throught and considered its wisdom across a variety of fields, from law and nursing to management development and education. Reflective journals are now an integral part of student life, even from early years. They work best when used on a daily or weekly basis to reflect honestly and critically on what has actually been learned during that period, and it helps stamp any learning on the memory so it's more likely to be utilized in the future.

The philosopher and psychologist John Dewey defined the term 'reflective thought' in the context of learning and education – the careful consideration of any belief or knowledge and the evidence around them. He believed that the general habit of self-reflection was important to be able to learn well. Although it's important to think about what was learned and how it was learned, the connections that were made to other information (past, present or future) also really mattered and would enable more options to become available. When journalling is used to capture the thinking, more cognitive strategies are used.[5]

## CONTINUOUS PROFESSIONAL IMPROVEMENT

This process of analysis, feedback and growth is what I call continuous professional improvement. As you question what you know, and integrate that with information or experience both old and new, you inevitably gain insight about what you don't know or hadn't noticed. Boud, Keogh and Walker, in their model of reflective learning, said that we must include our emotions in such reflection as they are central to learning – and the learning is then deeper because it is not simply an intellectual exercise.[6] Sociologist Jack Mezirow (1997) said that transformational learning takes place when we question our assumptions about what has happened and ourselves, so we become aware of how these constrain our understanding of the world.[7] The time spent reflecting means future decisions are then informed by any new understandings.

Journalling has also proved to be useful if someone goes through the stress of losing their job. A year-long experiment to see if journalling would have any effect on life after redundancy found that journalling allowed people to address their emotions, attain closure, gain new perspective and influence their attitudes about securing new employment.[3] In fact, it was so effective the experiment was actually discontinued after four months as it was no longer needed. He found that even though all involved were using an outplacement service, filling in forms and writing letters, those who wrote about the emotions around the redundancy were getting jobs at a much higher rate (68.4 per cent amount those who did compared to 27.3 per cent of those who did not).

## TRANSFORMATION TAKES EFFORT; EVEN BUTTERFLIES KNOW THAT

So you can see that if you're interested in personal and/or professional development, or in finding a job (or finding a job where you fit best), then taking the time to reflect is worth its weight in gold to you. If you're a natural reflector, journalling will give structure to your thinking and stop you simply ruminating, so you gain insight. At the other end of the spectrum, if you're an activist, then it's equally important to take the time to reflect, to stop every now and again and see if what you're about to jump in and do is the next best step for you. Transformation takes effort; even butterflies know that.

Once people understand this, most will make the effort to reflect as they want to do the best job they can. They want to be better than who they already are, or better at what they do in most areas of their life, whether that is work or a hobby they are interested in or passionate about. (Perfectionists, on the other hand, want to be perfect as well as being perfect in what they do, which puts immense strain on them and is entirely unnecessary, as I've learned, to be happy; 'Would I rather be perfect or happy?' is not a difficult question to answer.)

## PERFECTIONISM

I am a recovering perfectionist and now have a personal philosophy of continuous personal improvement that is more sensibly balanced towards the happiness end rather than perfection. I'm curious about how others do things better and I'd much rather learn from someone else's experience than personally learn the lesson myself as it's less painful that way. I call it personal development, some people call it self-help, but it is now part of who I am, wherever I am. I don't just do it at home and not at work, though I've found that the phrase 'self-help' generates strong reactions, including, 'I don't do self-help'. Well, I *do* 'do self-help', for if I can't help myself then I'm in a bad way, and I'd rather help myself where I can than rely on others to do what I could do myself.

Since I want to do the best job I can, I've often reflected on my performance and sought feedback. Sometimes, I didn't like the feedback at all – and in my worst job ever, I didn't accept much of what I was told and still wouldn't. (This was a job that completely – and unexpectedly – conflicted with my values at nearly every level, and it was there I found how effective journalling, and gratitude journalling in particular, was.) Not all organizations can afford executive coaching, but you can use your journal to help yourself in the following ways.

It has been shown that emotive writing helped sporting performance, but the same principle ripples out to work.[8] If you're fortunate, you could keep your work journal and review it with a coach on site or your own manager, but even if you just use it as a reflective journal, you're still going to benefit from it. If you are a manager, using a journal will help with self-awareness and remind you that the people you manage are probably having very similar conflicts, challenges or dreams. I'd also encourage you to get your team to start using journals so they can see what they want to discuss with you in more depth or understand what they might want to work on themselves.

## GOAL SETTING AND PROJECT MANAGEMENT

You will have goals that you need to meet that are set by the organization and you will have personal goals you want to achieve in your job. Somewhere along the line these need to coincide, otherwise there will be such a conflict that you will be unhappy in your work. Focusing on the key goals is what will bring success, because in any given role there will be numerous things you could focus on that in the end are really only distractions or, ultimately, unimportant. A journal allows you to look at any goal and break it down into smaller, achievable steps to ensure success.

## VALUES

Determine your values; it is important to spend time figuring out what these are. Your values need to coincide with those of your workplace; failure to ensure this happens is a fundamental reason for stress. Yet sometimes people don't really know what their values are now (as they can change over time) or they can't quite explain them – until someone overrides them. Being aware of your values means you know where your limits are: you know what you will and will not accept, and learn how to harness your own values to do your job with passion.

## TIME MANAGEMENT

Manage your time effectively. I don't think there's an easier tool to help you manage your time than journalling, mainly because it helps you see where you are wasting time and because it helps you focus on what you want to do. You can use it to create effective to-do lists, capturing the information that is whirling around in your head down on paper, rather than draining energy from you. Once written down, you can see what you must do and where you must delegate, and decide what is urgent and what is important, as Stephen Covey said (*see page 35*).

## STRESS

For different reasons, the modern workplace can be stressful, whether that is because of the demands of the job, the environment, the amount of control you have over what you do or changes in the workplace or externally, the threat of job losses, the amount of support you get, the resources you have available, workplace relationships and significant legislative changes on the horizon. Journalling is a significant benefit to stress and mental health (*see pages 165–70*).

## MANAGING STAFF AND APPRAISALS

Appraisals are the part of a manager's job that often takes the most time while generating the most problems after that hour-long conversation. Significant interpersonal skills are required to communicate effectively with people, particularly where performance, conduct or attitude need to be addressed. Feedback is critical in any system, and none of us like to feel we are being criticized, so when it goes wrong, it goes badly wrong. When feedback is given, you can choose to accept it or reject it, or take some of it on board, and it's a sign of maturity to be able to do this without defensiveness. Journalling can help you prepare for the conversations and reflect on the feedback given or received, and from it, develop action plans.

## PERSONAL DEVELOPMENT PLANS

As you reflect, you become aware of skills you need to develop or enhance for your new role, or where there are gaps you need to fill to ensure you have flexibility to move when the time is right. Identifying gaps means you know what you need to do next. Use it too to consider what a job *must* give you to be happy in it and to help you determine what you want from it.

## OTHER PEOPLE

There are very few jobs that don't involve working with other people. Sometimes, you just may not get on with certain people in the workplace and to a degree that's fine. You don't need to be friends, just professional. Yet if you are managing a difficult employee or working with someone who perhaps isn't working as part of a team, you need to find ways to deal with that other than simply reacting or withdrawing. Using your journal to observe that person and what interests them, how others interact with them, or how they interact with others, can be really helpful in showing you different angles to try and get an effective working relationship in place. It will also help you when you find yourself dealing with a new employee – or a new manager, with a quite different style than the one you were used to (or found yourself working easily with).

## CAREER DEVELOPMENT

You may move up, down or sideways in your organization, you may move out of it entirely to another company, or you may start your own. If you're feeling disgruntled or unhappy in your current job, you may think that this is no longer the career for you, when in fact, sometimes, all you need to do is change companies, roles or sectors to find your passion again. At other times, perhaps all you need to do is to think about the job you've been in for a while and remember the times when you were happy in what you did, and found meaning in aspects of it, to see exactly what it is that is missing that you need to find again. Or you may decide that what you need to do is change your attitude and stop focusing on the negatives in your role; find the positives and focus on those instead. The key thing to be happy in your job is to find meaning in it, a meaning that is in line with your values and even your higher purpose.

# Transform your professional life

**1** How do you feel about your work?

**2** What values are you able to express in your work?

**3** What could you do to develop your career?

**4** What is your next step and what skills do you need to develop for that?

**5** Do you feel stuck? If so, in what area? What options do you have?

**6** What career choices are available?

**7** What would be your dream job?

## Questions to reflect on at the end of each day:

**1** What did you learn today?

**2** What did you learn about yourself today and about who you want to be?

3  What could you have done better?




4  What challenges did you face that you need to work on?




5  What were you proud of today?




6  Did you treat people the way you wanted to treat them?




7  What would you rather have been doing today?

'Grief is a wise teacher. Grief teaches us that there is so much to know about ourselves and the world around us. Grief teaches us that we need to pay attention, to simplify our lives to be open to giving and receiving love.'

*Dr Alan D. Wolfelt,*
*grief expert and counsellor*

# 6 *Process grief*

## We all die and grief follows

Death is something that comes to us all and we should live our lives conscious of that fact. We need to do what we need to do to live well and to have good endings with the important people in our lives, because one day, they won't be there. We can't afford to wait to resolve issues, to tell someone we love them, as we've no idea when death will visit. And with death, comes grief; it is the price we pay for love, but we don't want it to cost more than it should by adding regrets to it.

Much of grief is an inside job. It's a solitary walk on a road you never asked to be on and to process it well is vital if we are to learn to live well again.

## GETTING STUCK

No two people deal with grief in the same way. Even within a family, or a group of people who loved the same person, there will be great differences in responses, some moving through grief, others finding loss cannot be surmounted. There are so many reasons why people get stuck. Sometimes it is about resilience.

At other times, it might be underlying beliefs about the ability to bear pain or that moving beyond loss means you are disloyal to the person who is gone. Or it could be trying to ignore or numb pain because moving forward means you must acknowledge the reality that a death has taken place, or that your own life is finite.

## GRIEF AS A TEACHER

Losing a loved one opens us to loss and great pain and changes out lives forever, but if we are not careful, we can get stuck in the past or in certain stages of the grief process because we fear loving anyone again. When we get stuck, we risk living a half-life where we close off our ability to love again – and then part of us is dead already.

## DEATH IS NEVER ACCEPTABLE, YET WE NEED TO ACCEPT IT

I have known people who remain stuck in a grey world where they see no light; who torture themselves with the unanswerable questions of 'why' and 'what if'; who resist help from friends and professionals and who make the decision to live only with loss. Equally, I have known people who have suffered great losses who decided they would not be stuck in 'this huge black tunnel' that seems like 'hell right now' (as my friend Diana defined it). They could accept death as something that could not be changed – and though that didn't make death acceptable, it meant connections could be made between the old and the new that enabled them to discover who they were now, to find purpose again, and sometimes even to live their lives with joy and positivity. Although Diana had always journalled, she came to see its real benefits when she suffered the traumatic and senseless loss of her husband. When she reviewed some of her early journals, she used to give her grief a name and called it 'the Greys' and when it was really painful it was 'the Grey Goblins'. Now, she says that colour in the world is important to her, because it is a sign of healing. In reviewing her journals, she could see that colour re-entered her world, partly helped by her Glad Book, where she recorded any little thing in that made her glad.

Lorna McLean lost her 17-year-old son. Without her loss, she says, 'I wouldn't have the voice that I have to share the wisdom that I carry. It's given me great courage, as you think, how am I going to survive this? There are things that happen in our life [and we wonder] how am I going to survive those? I can't get any lower, I can't fall any deeper. I can't be any more broken – and suddenly something happens and it starts – very, very slowly, one tiny step at a time, one breath at a time – and you suddenly find you've lived through something, or you are living through something – and therein lies the courage. The courage to take that step forwards and be able to say, "I've actually survived this".' She also says that now, looking back, there is 'so much joy – so much fun to draw on.'

## PROCESSING GRIEF

Journalling benefits those who have lost a loved one, as it helps to process grief, come to terms with the reality of that loss and mourn it.[9] You can use simple journalling techniques, such as recording how you are feeling or observing the stages you feel you are at, to see if you are moving forward or might need additional help. You can write letters to the person you have lost, or even write a letter as if it is from them, as a response to the letter you wrote. It's also a place to record your loss, the special memories you had (and why those matter), when you may feel no one else understands or no longer wants to listen. Later on, when you review your journey – for it must be a journey that takes you forward – you will have a record of change even where you believed none had happened, and you will even remember things that made you feel better so you can do them again.

In writing out grief, you can learn to transform pain so you see it as part of a life that goes on and where you can still be happy (but it's a different happy or happier), as indeed the person you have lost would have wanted you to be. Though death always changes us, it does not have to be something that defines you or ends more than one life. Using a journal through such times is one of the most powerful things that can be done in helping you take back a sense of control and though the landscape may be wholly changed, you will find you can survive and live, not exist.

It doesn't prevent the reality or the pain. In fact, if anything, the pain may become slightly worse as you start, but you need to bear with it and persevere in order to help change the thinking and emotions that are so often caught up in fear and a combination of memories and assumptions about the future or other people. The power of journalling is that it will stop an ever-downward spiral, help you work through the pain and ensure that you look after yourself at a time when you may feel there is no point in doing that. Research has shown it is a really useful tool to help you practice self-care as you fully honour yourself and your endings and beginnings, so use it.[9–10]

Cathy Rentzenbrink wrote about how, as a family, they needed to live with the aftermath of an accident that ultimately led to the decision to turn off her brother's life-support after eight years. The book *The Last Act of Love* prompted many to contact her and share their own sadness, but she felt that listening to this was too sad as it didn't show that you could learn to live well, and it didn't offer the hope she knew existed. As a result, she wrote *A Manual for Heartache*.

She defines heartbreak as the moment of impact, the rupture, the point at which everything changes and heartache is what you are left with. The content of the grief is always unique to the person involved; it's not possible to say you understand how someone feels as you can't compare experiences. But the process that one goes through to grieve – how you deal with it – is shared and you can learn from others. When Cathy was feeling well, she had access to this wisdom; when she wasn't, she couldn't, so she felt she needed somewhere to capture the information and the book grew from that. It is a reminder that there are good experiences and there are ways of thinking that lift a mood and help, not just grief, but depression too. The key is not to let emotions build up and to find helpful ways to let go of emotions like sadness, anger or fear. What she talked about was the difference between owning emotions and feeling them and about practising gratitude. Cathy also talked about how powerful she had found journalling to keep her healthy.

# Process grief

I remember when we …




My best memory of you is …




What am I denying?




What am I angry about?




Today, my grief looks like, sounds like, feels like …

I want you to understand …

The first time I …

My grief journey looks like …

I have learned that …

What have I accepted?

Six months from now, I hope …

## Questions to help use the power of rituals:

**1** What rituals could you introduce to honour your loss?

**2** How could you remember key dates like birthdays, weddings, etc.?

**3** What might help you move forward or let go (balloons, letters written and burned)?

**4** What could help you remember your loved one daily (candles, jewellery, art)?

## Choose a thought to concentrate on from the choices below:

I release fear and hold onto and honour the love we shared.

I can transform my pain and start creating a new reality where all is well.

# 7 Manage change

'A wise man adapts himself to circumstances, as water shapes itself to the vessel that contains it.'

*Chinese proverb*

## Stand up for your life

I used to believe that I was a hostage to fate and that I couldn't change what happened to me. In 2002 I read Cheryl Richardson's book, *Stand Up for Your Life*, and it was to set me off on a transformational journey where I found I could change my reality and learn from all that happened to me, including the events that were my responsibility or that I was partially responsible for. I also learned I would swim, not sink, and that led me to new jobs that were great (and sometimes awful, yet would prove to be huge learning spaces) to becoming a Reiki Practitioner, a Master NLP Practitioner and Master Hypnotherapist, an NLP Storyteller, a Justice of the Peace, a reader of thousands of books, a coach, workshop leader and speaker, poet and author. What I quickly learned was that how I handle change now affects my future, whether that is a change beyond my control or one I decide to make myself.

## THE CHANGE CONTINUUM

There's a continuum of how people handle change. It goes from one end, where there is no appetite for change (or indeed it may be feared or detested), where someone stays in the same house/job/relationship for years (even when they have outgrown them) through to those who throw themselves fully into change and actively and constantly seek it out. The rest of us are somewhere in between. My own personal experience of change, and my observations of how others deal with it in the workplace, made me curious about how journalling could help in this area, as well as on a personal level.

## WHY WE BEHAVE THE WAY WE DO

My background is primarily in Human Resources, which isn't just about policy and processes; it's also about the psychology of why people behave the way they do and how that affects organizations. Employees are more likely to be in a job that makes them happy, one that utilizes their abilities, in an organization that fits with their values and aspirations. Even with the best fit on both counts, the flexibility to change behaviour is the key to ongoing success. An organization can do its best to organize and plan for the external changes they feel are needed, but they are limited by the degree of influence they will have on individuals who may need to adapt to facilitate those changes. Where this isn't communicated or managed well, or where appropriate support is not given, the employee will disengage.

That is why so many engagement initiatives fail, because companies know what they want, say they know what their staff want, yet don't get to the bottom of what motivates the individual to build that into the communication and plans around the change. Individuals and teams need to see what value the change has for them, and not everyone wants to do that, so the organization must find ways to encourage as many people as possible to buy into the change and to believe it is as good for them as it is for the company. Ultimately, to do that means they have to change how people think – but do you know how you think? Do you know where you are on the continuum of change, or how flexible you are to adapt to changes?

## CONSCIOUSLY OBSERVING THOUGHTS

You can only work out exactly how you think by consciously observing your thoughts. Once you start, you may be surprised, because until you start trying to see things differently, you tend only to see what you 'see'. This is why brainstorming is often used as a tool when dealing with change, to try and find out what peers really think or feel, as well as to bring new ideas to the fore that others might not have considered.

## HELPING OTHERS DEAL WITH CHANGE

An effective way of helping people deal with change in the workplace is to encourage everyone to journal about the change itself as well as how they feel about it. If they are then encouraged to share most of their findings with the team, or manager, in a non-judgemental atmosphere, the honest discussion that ensues makes it easier for everyone. It is this combination of facts and feelings that makes the difference. Every health initiative deals in facts, but few lead to lasting or significant change until they tap into emotions and the individuals see the benefits of change and feel they can make that change in the community or family they live in.

## PERSONAL CHANGE

If you are going through personal change, then journalling provides a means to capture your thoughts, including the ones you might want to otherwise deny. Trying to deny what you really feel or think never works.

Taking the time to observe your thoughts means you can then address them and find a more helpful way to think. It's about changing the attitudes you bring to the situation, focusing more on the positive than the negative (but managing the negative as you can't ignore that either!). Where you identify a way of thinking that is less than positive, it can be helpful to identify an opposite belief that is stated in the present tense and that speaks about how you will handle the change, to use as an affirmation (a repeated phrase that changes your neural pathways over time even if you don't initially believe it at the start). If you are convinced the thought is a fundamental belief that you can't change, then you could create possibility of change by asking 'What if I could change the thought?' and write down your insights.

## KNOW WHAT YOU BELIEVE

Understanding what we believe and don't believe is a critical element in change because even the language we use can define, shape or reflect our beliefs, experiences and life. The words we use to express ourselves make a significant difference to how we feel, because our emotions, memories, assumptions and behaviours are all gathered among them.

## LISTEN TO YOUR LANGUAGE

If you're interested in personal development or behavioural change, start noticing the language you use on a regular basis; you will soon see you create your reality by the words you use. I was drawn to NLP because of its focus on language and its emphasis on excellence and facilitating change, often by making small adjustments to our thoughts and emotions, our senses and the representational systems we use to define them, which is what gives our experiences meaning. Here's an example. If I asked you to tell me how you saw life, what word would you use? Would you say that it's one darned thing after another, that it's scary, a struggle? Or would you say that life is an adventure, a joy, a privilege? If you hold the belief that life is a struggle, guess what? It's going to *be* a struggle, because that metaphor is a basic belief, and since our nature is to find evidence to back up our beliefs, then that is what you are going to see. To develop resilience and help people move forward, language needs to focus on the present and future, with reassuring phrases used like, 'You are coping remarkably well, and every week I can see a real change.' So if you want to change, change your words as you change your thinking – and change your life.

# Manage change

1 What belief or thought would you like to change most?

2 What evidence do you already have that this is not always true?

3 What change are you resisting?

4 Why are you resisting the change?

**5** What are you afraid of with respect to this change?

**6** What will it cost to keep things as they are?

**7** What benefits might the change bring?

**8** What changes in attitude and action are you committed to for the improvement of your quality of life?

**9** Whose feelings are you sparing by changing who you are?

**10** Whose feelings are you sparing by staying as you are?

**11** In which circumstances do you keep the peace rather than rock the boat?

## Choose a thought to concentrate on from the choices below:

'If nothing ever changed, there'd be no butterflies.' *Anon*

As I move through change, I remember to go gently, and take care of myself well.

# 8 Trust your own wisdom

'As soon as you trust yourself,
you will know how to live.'

*Johann Wolfgang von Goethe*

### Help, I need somebody

Are you always looking for the answers to your questions elsewhere? The answers to the big questions like, 'Why we are here?' and 'What career should I take?' or 'What sort of partner do I want?', and the seemingly smaller questions like 'What step do I take next?' Do you run from course to course, read book after book, check in with a hundred friends to get their opinion and then, weeks later, ask them again what thoughts they might have on what's been bothering you? If so, you've forgotten to trust your own wisdom and gut, and in the busy-ness of life, forgotten to listen to your heart.

The noise of others and the demands of the world can drown out our own still, small voices. We flit from thing to thing, person to person and leader to leader, looking for something yet always only searching for the words of peace that lie inside us. Not listening to what we really want to do, or not making decisions where our heart and head are in conflict, leads to stress and anxiety.

## YOUR OWN STILL, SMALL VOICE

Believe it. You have a voice inside of you that nothing can drown out, though it may be silenced for a while, or it might not have space to whisper loud enough through the advisors, therapists and other outside wisdom you keep seeking. Though there is wisdom in opening your eyes for the truths that only others can show you, there is also wisdom in listening to and learning to trust your own wisdom.

You just need to let it out or find the space to hold it again. Journalling helps you tap into your inner wisdom. Start off small and you will find that instead of always relying on your friendly neighbourhood (or faraway) guru – or family or friends for that matter – for support and advice, you will learn to trust yourself to find the answers. You will find your own solutions, access your own inner wisdom and be counselled from your own mistakes.

## USING OUTSIDE SUPPORT

Of course there may be times when outside support is required – through counselling or coaching, from books or courses, or just running an idea or challenge past some trusted friends. You cannot always be wise, but when you learn the difference between support and wisdom, and realize that responsibility for your future lies with you, that understanding is where you step into your power. You become the hero of your own adventure. As you learn to trust yourself again, you are aware that you may make mistakes and that you will still be OK. You will find you can draw on the resources that are deep inside you and know that each adventure prepares you for the next, even if it is only in the lessons about what you don't want to do.

## YOU HAVE THE ANSWER INSIDE YOU

Believe me, it is powerful when you realize that many times you already know the answer to the question that you asked others about and it greatly reduces your anxiety while increasing your self-belief that you can handle life.

Next time you want to know the answer to something, get out your journal and brainstorm that question in no more than five minutes (without censoring anything, as you can review it afterwards), or ask yourself the same question every day for twenty-five days and see how the answers unfold. Start with the belief you have the answers inside you; hold an affirmation in your head like, 'I trust my inner wisdom to guide me and keep me safe', or 'My inner wisdom gets louder and louder as I practise' or 'My inner wisdom helps me find the solutions I need'. Know that you can do it. Know that you don't need to depend on any one external person or group to rescue you; you are already all that you need.

# Trust your own wisdom

1 What advice would you give yourself at this time in your life?
(Use a piece of paper or a blank journal if you need more space to write.)

2 What is really happening with _____?

3 What will move you closest to the path you want to be on?

4 If you are not seeing something that you should be seeing, what might that be?

5  How well are you listening to your soul – the part of you that knows what really matters?

6  What do you need most at this time in your life?

7  What do you need to know about _____?

8  What needs to change so you feel you are living authentically, peacefully, joyfully?

9  How can you connect to your heart?

**10** Where do you not trust yourself?

**11** What signals is your body sending you?

## Choose a thought to concentrate on from the choices below:

My inner voice is clear and strong.

My inner wisdom gets louder and louder as I practice listening to it.

# 9 Embrace imperfection

'Ever tried. Ever failed. No matter. Try again. Fail again. Fail better.'

*Samuel Beckett*

## We can expect perfection everywhere

There are two main ways we can struggle with imperfection. The first is in our expectations of how perfectly others should behave in general and/or towards us and others. This leads us to judge them, having opinions on talent show contestants, politicians, on something a colleague, neighbour or friend does, or what those in our family do (or don't do). Such judgement isn't the careful weighing up of facts that leads to balanced opinions or decisions, it is the kind of judgement that is usually negative. This can quickly become a habit that is less than totally useful or kind, even if it ensures we stay with our current tribe and are still accepted (because we act the way they do and agree the social norms). And it's unfair to expect higher standards of others than we have for ourselves — for truth is, it's the fact we never can reach perfection that keeps us endlessly trying to reach it.

The second factor is in how we judge ourselves and we do that in at least two ways. Our inner critic never ceases to judge and correct us — that is its favourite job.

Our inner critic tells us we don't quite meet the standards required (ours or those of others), and it reminds us that we're not good enough, or not to make a fool of ourselves. To be honest, most of us wouldn't allow our friends to speak to us the way our inner critic does – yet often, we're not even consciously aware of what it's telling us, as it's so ingrained. So we need to bring our conscious awareness to it in order to start making friends with it, and to counter what it says with facts.

## THE TYRANNY OF PERFECTIONISM

For those of us who are perfectionists, imperfection is never acceptable. Perfectionism is much more than someone wanting to do a really good job; it's a tyrant that continually asks the unobtainable and gives us no peace of mind as we obsess about what we've done and whether it was good enough, and beat ourselves up thinking about how it wasn't. Underlying all perfectionism is fear, fear of not measuring up (usually to impossible and unrealistic expectations), and fear of failure (which is often self-fulfilling because of those unreasonable standards). This is exhausting, taking up so much of our time and mental energy, and it can prevent us trying new things we would enjoy or be successful at because we tell ourselves there's no point in trying in the first place. Needless to say, this won't improve our wellbeing. Hewitt and Flett argue that it prevents us from flourishing, which is all about health and success.[11] Why would we do that to ourselves? Why would we live in such fear, limit our lives, not take risks or try new things; instead, we should use all our talents and shine, and be OK with aiming for excellence rather than perfection.

## START EMBRACING YOUR IMPERFECTION

What can we do to change this? In your journal, start by tracking what you are saying and thinking about others and yourself. It can be really enlightening to see particular judgements on paper and notice when you are judging, what you are judging, the emotions this produces, the words you are choosing to use. It can help you see that your willingness to judge others often makes you feel better by feeling superior – and it can then encourage you to get out and deal with the reasons you feel inferior, angry or upset. It can certainly help you to be kinder and show compassion when you see how hard you judge others for behaving the same way as you do, or how upset you feel at being judged by someone else when they don't know all the facts. When we are judging, we aren't being compassionate, and we aren't building or practising self-care or self-compassion.

I'm still learning to love imperfection. Brené Brown's book *The Gifts of Imperfection* has certainly helped (even though my introduction to it prompted a vehement reaction about how ridiculous it was to see any sort of gift in being imperfect!). I then started to read the book, and as books sometimes do, this one whispered to my soul. Here was someone writing what I was learning too: that authenticity is a hard walk and a conscious walk, but IF we are to be authentic, then we recognize we are always imperfect. We have failed. We will fail. We are failing. In all tenses, all the time. When we accept we are imperfect, we stop judging ourselves, we see our humanity and failures, and we learn to forgive ourselves and to live life from a place of worthiness in spite of, and because of, that humanity.

Brené calls this 'wholehearted living' and for her, this means, 'cultivating the courage, compassion and connection to wake up in the morning and think, "No matter what gets done and how much is left undone, I am enough." It's going to bed at night thinking, "Yes, I am imperfect and vulnerable and sometimes afraid but that doesn't change that truth that I am worthy of love and belonging."'

Judgement and vulnerability are words that do not sit easily together, so to be one, we must let go of the other. We might initially scream against the concept, but we find that letting go of perfectionism allows us to live with compassion for ourselves and for others, and that allows us to live in freedom, allows us to fly. We first need to start noting where and when we do this, and what we say to ourselves (or others). Then we need to challenge our judgements, looking for evidence to counter them (which may include thinking about the success that others have even though they submit work that is less than totally perfect), deciding that good enough is good enough and discovering what those new standards might look like. It could be to ask yourself questions about what you are really afraid of, or you could imagine what your 'perfection' would say – as if it was another person – to you about it's reasons (try writing this as a two-way dialogue). Or you might discover some root causes for perfectionism that lie in early relationships where you didn't feel accepted or approved of as you were, and then finding ways to move forward with that information. Whatever you do, do it without worrying about using the correct grammar or your best handwriting! Write, scribble, draw, paint or collage what you're thinking and tell yourself that it's all good, for it's hard to be truly creative when you keep judging as you go along. When you see some of your underlying beliefs and assumptions you may well be shocked that you feel that way, but be gentle on yourself and welcome the wisdom as now you can change your beliefs for something that doesn't limit you in the same way. It's all good – and good enough.

I'll leave the last word with Brené, who says, 'Perfectionism is the belief that if we live perfect, look perfect and act perfect, we can minimize or avoid the pain of blame, judgment and shame. It's a shield. Perfectionism is a 20-ton shield that we lug around thinking it will protect us, when in fact it's the thing that's really preventing us from taking flight.'

# Embrace imperfection

**1** When working on a project, ask yourself – could you survive the worst that could happen?

**2** Will what you are trying to make perfect still matter in three months' time?

**3** What beliefs do you have that have led to you being a perfectionist?

**4** How do you view mistakes?

5 Have others told you that you are too hard on yourself? Why might they say that?

6 Do you struggle to meet your own standards? How does that make you feel?

7 When do your standards get in the way of living the life you want to live?

8 How could you handle feedback better?

**9** What is the difference between perfection and excellence?

**10** Does your perfectionism honour you?

**11** Where could you start lowering your standards to realistic levels?

**12** What lessons have you learned about your failures?

**13** Who says you need to be perfect?

**14** What anxieties lie under your need to be perfect?

**15** What excuses do you use to protect yourself from failure?

## And:

Brené Brown says she carries around a piece of paper in her wallet that just has the names of the people whose opinions matter to her, those who care about her whatever stage of life she is in. On a sheet of paper, write down who would be on your list.

## Choose a thought to concentrate on from the choices below:

'Gold cannot be pure, and people cannot be perfect.' *Chinese Proverb*

All I can do is my best.

# 10 Communicate better with yourself and others

'The single biggest problem in communication is the illusion that it has taken place.'

*George Bernard Shaw*

## Breakdowns in communication

Communication is a two-way process that involves the sharing of information (factual, historical, visionary, feelings, beliefs) in many different ways and from a variety of sources. All the wars that have been fought, all the relationships that haven't worked out, and all the arguments you've ever had have involved a breakdown in communication at some point. Like me, you've probably suffered a few major communication issues, where things have escalated quickly in a direction you couldn't have imagined at the start of the conversation. There are many reasons this occurs, including:

- Misunderstanding what was said (sometimes intentionally).
- Hearing something that wasn't said at all.
- Being less than totally honest about what you feel or think.
- Telling lies.
- People assigning a meaning to the words, language or tone that is not there.
- Emotions involved where you feel threatened, fearful, hurt or unimportant.
- When you want to protect others.

## HOW WE ACTUALLY PROCESS COMMUNICATION

The Neuro-linguistic Programming Communication Model was one that made so much sense to me. Anything we process first comes to us via one of our senses, but then it goes through a number of different filters that change what we experience depending on a wide range of factors, including our personality, memories, physiology, the language we favour, as well as our environment, genes, values, attitudes and beliefs.

These filters will rarely just store that information as it is: they will delete things your mind decides aren't necessary; distort it based on all the other information it has or how you choose to think about things; or generalize it out through your experience, beliefs and values to draw global conclusions. Since the end results are always unique to the individual, it helped me understand why someone could react in an unexpected way to something that was said.

How we personally hold onto or process information affects our behaviours and emotions, and thereby impacts and shapes our values and beliefs – often at deep, unconscious levels. We may say or think one thing, or believe we are demonstrating or living precisely this, but the rest of our body tells a different story to those who know what to watch out for. There is no resonance. Our body language and eye movements, breathing rate, colour and tone cannot lie. The good news is that this shows how strong our desire to be real and congruent is; even when we try to deceive ourselves and others, our true nature, thoughts and feelings want and need to express themselves. When something someone is saying doesn't ring true, you can be sure at some level it isn't – for instance, when they reassure you that they want to make a change, but deep down they don't believe they can do it, you'll know it.

## WHY GREAT COMMUNICATION MATTERS

It's not just major communication breakdowns that cause us problems. We say things we immediately wish we could take back, we forget to share critical information and it can take some time and effort to undo the damage that is caused.

Communication is that simple – and that hard – so we can do with all the help we can get to improve it, given how fundamental it is to good relationships. Journalling really helps you do this, not least because you're communicating with yourself and joining all parts of you up (your logical brain to your emotions, feelings, beliefs and values, your consciousness to your unconsciousness). If you've tried beating yourself up after a conversation that didn't go that well – or where you've been given a different response than the one you had hoped for – it is useful to ask yourself questions about what happened. This time to reflect is something that can be useful in many other situations. By answering questions, you will often gain insight into what may be helpful to change, or an area that you should work on more. If this happens to me, I ask myself questions like:

- What happened there?
- Was I honest?
- Was I honest in a way that respected the other person?
- Why did I react in the way I did?
- Why might they have reacted in that way?
- When did I notice things starting to go wrong?
- What prevented me from saying what I knew I needed to say?
- What was done or said that made me feel the way I felt?
- And what WAS it that I was feeling?
- What will I do with this insight?
- What will I do or say differently if something similar occurs?
- How could I have improved what I said or how I said it?
- How can I start to mend things (if necessary)?

## HINDSIGHT INSIGHT

I've got great hindsight insight. I can go away after a particular interaction and reflect on it and kick myself for what I said, or mainly what I didn't say, or what I could have said better. I used to get really frustrated about my apparent inability to argue a point at the time, or when I would get tied up in knots by someone else's clever arguments or manipulation. Now though, I approach many of these questions with an attitude of curiosity about what I will find, as I know 'there is no failure, only feedback'. Now I speak directly and openly to people (so there are far fewer misunderstandings), I stand up for myself and others, I have joined Toastmasters, I write poetry, I am more observant when I speak to people and I am a better listener.

Taking this time out for reflection means I don't usually repeat the behaviours – or at least make the same mistakes again as often. There is great value in this kind of examination of our lives and so we should create the space to do it, because how we communicate is how we build relationships. It's also how we really get to know ourselves. It is too easy to forget what we believe or what is important to us. By not listening to that still small voice inside you, life may become a life lived in whispers or silence (or a life of aggressive confrontation). Take the time to find your voice and message. You'll find it sounds sweeter than you thought – and when you need to, you'll remember when it's time to roar.

# Communicate better with yourself and others

**1** In which circumstances are you not willing to hear the truth?

**2** Do you express yourself truthfully at all times and in all places?

**3** What have you left unsaid that you need to say now?

**4** What are you keeping to yourself that you should share with someone?

**5** What do you think will happen if you do speak up or speak the truth?

**6** Who do you need to apologize to for something you said, or how you said it?

**7** What do you need to listen to more?

**8** What do you say when you are asked how you would describe life? If that is less than totally positive, what is a better phrase or word to use?

**9** Write down examples of conversations that you want to have in real life.

10 When you next have a problem with communication, use the technique Toyota have used since the company's founder, Sakichi Toyoda, developed it in the 1930s. Called 'The Five Whys', it is a process to determine the root cause of a problem by repeating the question 'why?' five times in order to understand what is happening and develop a resolution.

## And:

Review this journal or another journal you keep and pull out ideas that need more development or thinking through and work on these – to develop your self-communication skills.

Start a family or couple journal, which sits out all the time and allows people to write how they are feeling, what they want or what they are grateful for.

## Choose a thought to concentrate on from the choices below:

The more I communicate my needs, the more I get what I want out of life.

People listen to what I say.

'You yourself, as much as anybody in the entire universe, deserve your love and affection.'

*Buddha*

# 11 *Be gentle on yourself*

## Being gentle with ourselves starts with our thoughts

Hand in hand with letting go of judgement and perfectionism must come self-compassion, or self-acceptance, however you like to define it. Perhaps you already know that you are extremely hard on yourself (usually because others keep telling you this is the case), or maybe you think this isn't an issue for you. I'd be surprised if it wasn't. Journalling can help you see how harsh you are being on yourself, particularly if you use a stream of consciousness technique (*see page 20*) where you just get what's inside out. I've said before that this is one of the best ways to deal with your inner critic; the protective mechanism that aims to stop you failing or getting hurt, but one that also stops you trying and learning, and keeps you living life small. By noting the negative comments and thinking on paper, you can start to acknowledge them, bring them into the light of day and no longer push them down and try to ignore them. And being gentle on yourself brings the realization that you no longer have to accept anything they say.

## Automatic Negative Thoughts

Psychiatrist Dr Daniel G. Amen calls these 'ANTS'. Automatic Negative Thoughts are part of our nature as they aim to protect us from failure and pain by straight away taking a negative position. He describes different varieties of thoughts like 'all or never thinking', 'catastrophic predicting', 'mind reading/assumptions', 'guilt tripping' and 'labelling' (i.e. 'You're such an idiot'). And like real ants, he says you need to learn to stamp on them because they are not true.

My brother uses a technique called 'Squish it, squash it, smile'. This isn't about squashing down the ANTS in the hope that they will go away, because when we do this, they will always find a way to resurface. Instead, we are to look at the thought, examine it to see if it's real, how it is making you feel and what the real issue might be or what memory it might be triggering. Then you can deliberately decide not to accept that the thought is true for you *now*. And you can smile for lots of reasons, including the fact that you are being gentle on yourself, and this automatically starts to make you feel better.

## SELF-COMPASSION

Life can bring many stressful situations to us, which can affect our wellbeing significantly. Research by Odou and Brinker (2014) showed that journalling is a better way to deal with emotions than simple distraction techniques, but it was important to be self-compassionate when dealing with them.[12] Most of us probably need some help here – and if you want to know what your baseline is, check it out at Dr Kristin Neff's website (*see page 208*). Dr Neff is an expert in this area and I'm honoured she's given me permission to use her work in my journalling workshops. Remember that you can't change what you don't acknowledge or understand, so spend the time doing the test and check out the wide range of resources she lists on the site too, and the exercises she suggests.

Other people write on the subject too and give very helpful guidance. Cheryl Richardson suggests we need to practice extreme self-care. In her book *The Art of Extreme Self-care*, she recommends planning ahead with a self-care 'first-aid kit'. This is a plan of action to use before we need it and that is really important, because when we are feeling less than totally great, it takes too much effort to think about what might help improve things. You can use your journal to figure out what you need to put in your own kit. She also provides a really helpful list of questions that allow you to assess what to add to your kit, which includes people who can support you, as well as ways to support yourself by letting go of some things while remembering to do others. I've been doing something very similar for years with a focus on what makes you feel better and/or contributes to your own happiness and wellbeing.

You don't necessarily have control over how others treat you – but you do have control over how you treat yourself. Take the time to journal your reflections on what it says, and how you would live your life differently if you really believed you were a child of the universe, as poet and scholar Max Ehrmann describes in his poem *Desiderata*, with a right to be here.

# Be gentle on yourself

**1** What nourishes you?

**2** Do you always put others' needs before your own? Why?

**3** How does what you do for a living reinforce your belief about how you live and how you nurture yourself?

**4** What are your obstacles to nurturing yourself?

**5** What are you tolerating in your life that you would like to change to improve your quality of life?

**6** List three internal and three external changes you'll need to make to ensure you nurture yourself.

7 What habits and behaviours do you have that stop you nurturing yourself well?

8 What is the one thing you could do that would strengthen your relationship with yourself?

9 Do you let your friends nurture you? Why not?

10 Who do you know who nurtures themselves well? How do they do this?

11 How do you know you are not nurturing yourself (physically, mentally, etc.)?

# 12 Choose victor over victim

'In the long run, we shape our lives, and we shape ourselves.'

*Eleanor Roosevelt*

**Feeling sorry for yourself leads nowhere**

Once upon a time, there was a Chinese stonecutter who was good at his job but had a chip on his shoulder about most things. He was full of self-pity about what had gone wrong in his life: at his lowly position, at the fact he hadn't had the same chances as other people; because he was robbed many years ago; because his wife had left him because he worked too hard. His resentment grew, fed by his self-pity. As this is a fairy story, the man got what he wished for: he wished he could be like the merchant, because he saw that the merchant was rich and powerful and could have anything he wanted — so he became the merchant. After a while, because this was the way he thought, the man began to feel sorry for himself once again, as he felt he didn't have enough power. He saw that the chief official had more power than the merchant, so he became the chief official.

But the man realized the Chief Official didn't have the most power, because he had to sit in his chair protected from the heat of the sun; therefore it must be the sun that had the most power. So the man became the sun, only to realize that the clouds were even more powerful as they could stop the sun shining on the people below. He felt sorry he was not the clouds and the next instant he became the clouds. But then he wished he was the wind, because the wind could blow the clouds wherever it wanted, and so he became the wind. But the wind could not move the stones the stonecutter had once worked on and the man finally realized how foolish he had been to wish his life away and feel sorry for himself; he asked if he could return to his work where, no longer wasting time feeling sorry for himself, he could create the things he had always wanted to create. I love this story!

## IT MATTERS WHERE YOU CAME FROM – AND IT DOESN'T MATTER WHERE YOU CAME FROM

Many years ago I became fascinated by the ways that people react to difficult circumstances. I would ask the experts why people reacted so differently to fairly similar events. I never received a satisfactory explanation, apart from the individual's genes, background and environment, even when these were also similar. One expert even told me that it came down to luck. This I could not accept, but it showed me they didn't really know.

Our background and environment are mainly external factors and epigenetics shows that we aren't even victims of our genes as much as we might think, as these are often mutable. I was sure that the reason wasn't simply down to our background or environment; it was what we did with these external factors internally – how we process an event, our thinking, beliefs, attitudes and values, and the choices we make as a result – that had most impact. An experience that is difficult for you may not be so for me, and vice versa, but what happens when we become stuck in such experiences or environments and allow ourselves to be defined by them? What happens when that becomes our only story? What happens when we aren't resilient enough, or are unwilling to take steps to build our resilience? This is too often where a victim mentality creeps in.

The danger lies where we begin to view life as a series of things that happen to us, over which we have no control, and that we have no control over how we think about these things. The 'bad' news is that we do have control over our thinking (this is bad news if you'd prefer to remain a victim). However, this is also the good news. We do not have to be defined by anything in particular or even life in general, and we can – and must – choose to move forward so we don't live with self-pity. Even a small change, like not using the word 'victim' can make a difference. I don't use the word 'survivor' either, as both terms keep you welded to that incident or person. Instead, I use words like 'warrior' or 'adventurer'.

## SELF-PITY IS SELF-DESTRUCTIVE

Self-pity keeps you focused on yourself and means you stay angry and resentful. The writer and social activist Helen Keller said, 'Self-pity is our worst enemy and if we yield to it, we can never do anything wise in this world.' In the longer term it is unwise and it exhausts us, because it establishes a pattern in which we refuse to accept responsibility for what happens next, for not taking power back, for not choosing to be a victim of circumstances.

Do we want to be defined by disappointments, mistakes and missed opportunities? Do we want to remain a victim of outside circumstances that we can't control, or do we want to take charge of as much as we can through the choices we make? Drama like this keeps life pretty interesting (and some people thrive on a constant stream of drama), but too often it is what keeps us stuck because we like the attention we get as a result, or we feel it allows us to stay where we are and tell the same stories; it improves our feelings of importance, or the fact that we are seen and heard on some sort of stage. It's time to end the drama and the predisposition to escape from reality and accept what is. It is time to stop being happy in our unhappiness.

## TAKE BACK YOUR POWER

As long as you continue to blame anyone or anything for where you are now, you will continue to feel powerless and live in fear.

If you are feeling fearful and powerless you must consciously act to change it, because action breaks the chains of fear every time. When we deliberately choose hope over fear, we are no longer powerless. Hope is not about feeling powerless – it's knowing you can do something that can change things for the better.

## REFUSE TO BE A VICTIM

Refusing to be a victim will set you free from resentment and anger – and ultimately set you free from those who caused the initial pain that you are still carrying around in your head. You will stop focusing on yourself, stop the self-pity that was keeping you stuck in a grey world – and you will start taking steps to be free from that burden. It's a conscious choice we must make in the middle of our own particular circumstances. The psychologist and writer Susan Jeffers has said that you show a victim mentality every time you give your power away to someone else; when you choose to be over-responsible and stay where you are; when you don't ask for help or take up offers of help; or when you expect others to make you happy or read your mind. This also sounds much like martyr behaviour.

Step into your power and own it; it is a powerful thing to face difficult situations and find ways to deal with them. If you are fed up with being a victim, if you know that self-pity has crept in, if you want to find reasons for more than survival, to break free or move forward, asking where you have victim mentality with an open heart will set you free. It's never too late to choose victor over victim.

# Choose victor over victim

Think of a particular situation that troubled you and then ask these questions:

1 When you think back to particular events that trouble you, what was your role in the situation?

2 If you are honest, do you enjoy the drama and attention the story gives you (either when you share it with others or when you talk to yourself about it)?

3 Could you be OK with not being the victim anymore?

**4** In which circumstances do you feel sorry for yourself?

**5** What in your thinking keeps you holding onto this event?

**6** How have you let this event define and shape your life to date?

**7** How can you take your power back?

8  What fears lie behind you remaining a victim?

9  How do you benefit from remaining a victim?

10  What coping strategies have you been using to date that need to change?

11  What gifts do you now have as a result of what happened?

## Choose a thought to concentrate on from the choices below:

I release myself now from feeling like a victim and choose my own future.

I have the right to be treated with respect and dignity.

'Everyone has been
made for some
particular work and the
desire for that work has
been put in every heart.'

*Rumi*

# *13* **Find your purpose**

**Your purpose is often not what you do for a living**

If someone was to ask you what the purpose of your life was, how would you answer them? Would you explain why you work in the job you do, or if you don't work, how you choose to spend your time? Let's be clear at the outset — having reasons to work is not necessarily the same thing as having a purpose.

Some people are born knowing their purpose; they have vocations or 'callings' to particular areas of work and filter out other options to allow them to do what they feel destined to do. Some people give no thought to this at all and go to work every day, living for what they do outside their job. Some let it cross their minds occasionally but are quite happy taking life as it comes and seeing where the wind takes them.

When someone knows who they are, they will do what makes their heart sing, and this can work to reveal their purpose anyway. Or they might 'accidentally' stumble on it through a series of adventures and steps. A search for purpose begins and ends with what makes you feel alive, passionate, in the flow, happy. This is the wisdom the poet and theologian Rumi shared when he counselled that you just need to 'let yourself be silently drawn by the stronger pull of what you really love.' Most of us will have a level of desire inside us to know why we are here and we will find this question popping up all the time, increasingly so as we get older. As the years pass, if we don't follow our joy, we find that we still can't really answer the question, 'What do you want to do when you grow up?'

## THE DRIVE TO FIND MEANING IN LIFE

Holocaust survivor Viktor Frankl said that we need to challenge our understanding of the meaning of life; it was this that allows us to be truly human.

The drive to find a meaning in life that is bigger than 'who you are now' or 'what you do to pay the bills' is what allows you to make a contribution, create a legacy, or leave the world in a better state than you found it. The one thing that won't work is waiting for inspiration. I don't mean that you shouldn't spend time in solitude or on retreat to give yourself space to hear what your heart tells you. Too often we wait for wisdom and clarity to fall into our laps when in fact we need to actively pursue the answer by finding what we love and doing more of that. As we start to discover what makes us excited, passionate, peaceful or happier, and as we follow the paths that open up before us, then synchronicity will start to work and we will begin to see markers on our path, meet exactly the right person, see the signs that are there, and it will become clear what our next step is. The good news is that we don't need to see the ending at the beginning. All we ever need to do is take the next step.

## BEING OPEN WILL LEAD YOU HOME

When you are open to seeing what is in front of you, when you are curious and willing to act, your purpose will be revealed. That's where your journal creates a magic all of its own so you can find all the answers you need. If this is something you are struggling with, then it might be an idea to use the back of your journal to note things that make you excited or curious, or that prompt strong emotions.

## WHAT WORKED FOR ME

Here's how I worked out my purpose in life. I sat with my journal and made an honest list of what I felt my unique personal qualities were. I also made a list of what inspired me, brought me to tears, made me angry or upset and kept me interested. The clues were there. I also sent out an email to some friends from various walks of life, using questions the writer Cheryl Richardson suggested, to ask them how they felt I had contributed to their lives, how I had been a teacher, how I had challenged them to grow or introduced them to something that meant they lived their lives differently. I was really scared to do it as I had to be open to an honest response (or to no response) – but I am so glad I did it. It showed me sides of myself that I wasn't aware of, and qualities that I didn't appreciate, but others did.

I spent time reflecting without censoring what I was thinking, without batting away ideas or telling myself I was being boastful, without worrying about what other people might think. Determined to be real, I identified patterns and key themes over many years and spent time answering questions on those themes to find out where else they had been evident and where I had expressed a particular quality. I pursued the answers, sitting with them until I was sure they really were my answers. Not what I thought I should be doing with my life, or what someone thought I should be doing.

Soon two things became clear. I saw that words were very important to me. I am a life-long lover of books and poetry and believe words can influence people deeply. My own life had been changed by reading Cheryl Richardson's book *Stand Up for Your Life*. I realized that these particular words – 'inspire', 'encourage' and 'empower' – were qualities I had and that I admired and appreciated in other people too. They resonated with me, there was a nod of my head as I recognized this, and when I put my hand on my heart or my stomach, I felt peaceful, joyful and determined to do what it took to ensure I lived in a way that reflected them.

I'd found the qualities that really mattered to me, but I wasn't sure how to turn them into a 'purpose'. I started to think about what really mattered to me and what my ideal world would look like. I knew respect and kindness were such fundamental values that they would be expressed whatever I did, so I was looking for other qualities that mattered – like everyone being loving, inspired to live their best lives, where they were encouraged to do that, and assisted and empowered others to do the same. I then created a statement to summarize this: I want to use my words to inspire, heal, encourage and empower others to live the life they want.

The interesting thing is that at the time I wrote this summary, I actually wasn't feeling that inspired, encouraged or empowered myself. I was in a job I hated because of its culture and how people were treated, but I felt stuck because of personal circumstances. I'd forgotten to do what made me happier but perhaps because I was feeling disempowered and lost, with no voice, I was determined to change and find ways to change.

Once I'd defined my purpose, this really helped me determine goals. Deciding to do what helped me stay focused, persevere, overcome obstacles, examine the way I was living, figure out what was working and wasn't working – and say no to anything that didn't sit with where I felt I was going. It also helped me to have the courage to say yes; yes to stepping out into my light knowing that living in the shadows, fearing what others might think, or playing small and quietly does not serve the world.

## LIVE LIFE LARGE

Refuse to live small when you decide to figure out your own purpose. Think back to times in your life when you felt 'in the flow', when things were going fantastically well, when you absolutely knew you were passionate about something. Then come up with some suggestions that will help you see where the real passions in your life lie. Don't censor what you think your purpose might be. Stay calm by focusing on your strengths. Step into your light, know your purpose and live it.

# Find your purpose

1 What are you naturally good at?

2 What do you do that makes you lose yourself so you forget about time?

3 Who and what inspires you?

4 If people ask you for help, why do they ask? What is it that you uniquely give?

5 If you knew you would be successful and happy in your work regardless of what anyone else thought – and had enough money (whatever the definition of 'enough' is for you) – what would you be doing?

6 If you were writing your obituary, what is the one thing you would regret not doing/being/having?

7 Why are WE here? What do you see as the purpose of life or humanity?

8 How do you want to contribute to the world?

9 What hidden potential do you have that you aren't using?

10 Do you feel that you have a lot of potential that's still hidden?

**11** What do you keep talking yourself out of?

**12** What excuses do you use not to follow your dreams?

**13** Is life a choice between working for money or working for the love of what you do?

**14** If you know what your purpose is, are you wholeheartedly living it?

## Choose a thought to concentrate on from the choices below:

Today, I will make choices that honour my purpose in life.

I am free to discover what my purpose is and live it.

# 14 Access your creativity

'Stillness is where
creativity and
solutions are found.'
*Meister Johann Eckhart*

**We are all creative**

In *The Gifts of Imperfection*, Brené Brown writes about how she had become completely disconnected from her creativity, believing that she had a 'real job' instead. For her, it was one definition or the other. Like many of us, she remembered her attempts at art in school being criticized by a teacher or school friends. Did you give up on creativity as a child? That doesn't mean you aren't creative.

When we think about creativity, too often we think about those who create great works of art, music, literature or engineering and know we don't have the genius to do such things. We focus on perfection or standards that were never meant for us — and in search of that perfection, we do nothing. We forget that some who call Shakespeare a genius do not see the genius in Ralph Waldo Emerson, Jane Austen, Rumi, Jean-Michel Basquiat, Yo-Yo Ma, Handel, Jon Bon Jovi or David Bowie. Some find Monet and Turner amazing and others only collect Warhol.

Yet creativity is found everywhere you go and the evidence is all around you: it's in the phone you use, the car you drive, the kitchen and equipment you choose, the clothes you wear, how you decorate your home, the public spaces you use, the music you listen to and the books you read. All of these were just ideas at one time – but the idea needed to come first, and then someone needed to use their creative gifts and be inspired to bring them to life.

Many people express their creativity in their job or hobby. They make beautiful ceramics, amazing photographs, jewellery, gardens or garden furniture, cars, homes and interiors, or cakes, write poetry, create music or sing. A large number, however, have blocked their creativity, perhaps because they have shut down in some areas of their life (which has a knock-on effect on everything else they do), or they are thinking like a child and recalling what parents or teachers said about doing something more important instead, or they won't create because it will never be good enough (just as they are never good enough; beliefs generalize out, remember).

Perhaps one of these rings true for you, or perhaps you are just too tired to be creative, too caught up in the cares of life that you have even forgotten to appreciate the beauty around you, let alone create any.

## CREATIVITY IS A PRIORITY

As a child, I was always creating artwork and poems. I stopped doing it all, using many different excuses. Then at some point, I just forgot about expressing it at all. Life got busy, I had different priorities at different times. I had four children who were under five to look after and an elderly aunt, a father who was dying, various community or church activities, two jobs and a degree to study for. I buried my creativity so deeply (or perhaps buried myself so deeply) that I thought it had gone forever. Does that sound familiar? Well, the good news is that it never disappears; it just resurfaces in different forms. Though sometimes it's easier to disconnect from beauty and possibility than it is to hold onto it. Even when creativity is exactly what we should be trying to keep hold of and focus on, we choose to box it up instead, making everything else a priority. It isn't just our lives that are poorer for doing that, as often our creativity impacts others.

When we smother it, our creativity doesn't just lie there quietly, because it is fundamental to who we are. It keeps trying to catch our attention, allowing us to be drawn to things we are inspired by, forcing us to rest so we have time to think about things again, feeling upset by something someone else has created that we had once planned to do. To kick-start my creativity, I started by writing in my journal; I needed to reconnect with my own creativity, and to figure out what that now meant. As ideas started to take shape, I found myself going on mosaic courses, writing a blog, creating word butterflies for friends, writing letters, starting Facebook groups, writing poetry to deal with my emotions or help others – and found that I was creating meaning in my life in a way that was truly unique to me. My contribution to the world, however small, still improved the world – or, at least, it improved me.

Albert Einstein said imagination was more powerful than knowledge. Journals help us imagine, dream again, explore in a safe environment, then try things out and allow the feedback to help us grow and create better things.

Imagine using your journal to remember what it is to play. Then record the various ideas this inspires and simply create the space to be creative.

## OFFERING OUR CREATIVITY TO THE WORLD

Creativity is vital for everyone. Sir Kenneth Robinson is an internationally recognized leader and consistent advocate for creativity. Much of what he writes and speaks about is how our education system stifles children's natural creativity and imagination, and how this fails our children, their teachers and, ultimately, society. He says creativity cannot be standardized because we are all human beings with personal preferences that have to be taken into account. He argues that without this creativity, we, the places we work and the world in which we live, are impoverished. And he's right.

In the workplace, innovation is critical, because of the speed with which companies and technology change. To allow for this, the modern workplace will need to be one that allows risks, allows time to let imagination flow and has the determination to follow the ideas through. The best companies build in downtime for their employees as part of their working day and encourage them to take all of their holidays. As an individual, you need the same, so it is critical to make the time to nurture this. You create time for everything else in your life that is important to you – so no more excuses. Learn to trust the creative process and yourself.

# Access your creativity

1 How or where can you be more playful, or take more risks?

2 How do you distract yourself so you don't have time to be creative?

3 What do you want to create that is unique to you?

4 What inspires you? What senses are most affected? What moves you to tears or strong emotions?

5 What part does perfectionism play in you not using your creativity?

**6** What can you do to build a creative environment around you?

**7** How can you deliberately make time to be creative?

**8** What did you used to love to do as a child?

**9** Who inspires you? If you were to see/hear/think like them, what might happen next?

And, on a sheet of paper or in a blank journal:
Write a list of one hundred things you might enjoy doing or might try.

In the context of your creativity, fill in ten answers to this question:

I wonder what would happen if _____?

# 15 Change your story, change your life

'We do not deal much
in facts when we are
contemplating ourselves.'
*Mark Twain*

## What story are you telling just now?

Your reality — how you are living your life at the moment — is based on the story you are telling yourself about what it should look like, or at least on the story you've told to date. You don't believe me? Well, consider this. Many of your fears, dreams and hopes come from your past experiences or from fears about your future based on what you already know or imagine. You cannot change your past; running from it, trying to forget it by numbing it or carrying it with you all the time will not change it. Even if you took the extreme step of disappearing from where you are and reinventing yourself somewhere else, the likelihood is that you would still be using your past to build your future, if you are holding onto it too tightly. Ultimately, it is what you tell yourself about the past that makes the difference, because this is your story. You are the story-teller, and realizing that *you* create your reality from your stories means taking responsibility for the story you tell if you want to live your best life.

Ever since I was little, I have loved stories, and I still do. I'd finished all the books in our school library by the time I was eight years old and my teacher used to cycle five miles to the nearest library to bring me a basket of books that I would devour, so by the time I was eleven, I'd read many of the classics. When I wasn't reading or playing in the park opposite our house, I usually lived in daydreams that were sometimes fun, but mostly an escape and a waste of time and energy. I also had memories of my maternal grandmother telling me stories of ghosts and banshees and fairies, many of which she believed to be true.

## WHY WE CREATE OUR STORIES

I didn't come across the concept of how our personal story holds us back until I read the work of Don Miguel Ruiz (and once I'd been introduced to the concept, of course I saw it everywhere). I realized how important it was that we took control of something we did naturally. We all have a story; it is made up of our experiences, our feelings, our thoughts, hopes and dreams. Our story – how we got to where we are now – is like any other story, but when we tell it (to others or ourselves), we forget that we are choosing which parts we focus on, how particular events ended, or what other people were doing or thinking. We are deeply inclined to hold onto our stories of pain, rejection and failure. I often ask people on my courses to make a timeline of significant events in seven-year periods (or decades) of their lives and then ask them to tell me what percentage of those events were positive things; the answer is never above 10 per cent. This tendency means we still hold onto the people or events that caused us pain, the people who rejected us, or our failures (so we fear trying again). Unfortunately, we don't just hold onto the stories. Too often, we also hold onto the memories and the feelings connected to those stories. Over time, this can lead to increasing anger, a desire for revenge, feelings of hopelessness and depression. Understanding the emotions involved in the stories we tell is vital.

## HOW YOU TELL YOUR STORY MAKES THE DIFFERENCE

Dr James Pennebaker argues that storytelling simplifies complex experiences and that the stories we tell about ourselves are actually what help us understand those events better, even when they are traumatic. But his research shows that it is how you tell your story that makes the difference to your future. When we can change the emotions attached to a story, or focus on a different part of the story or a different story altogether, then we subtly change the story – and that can change our lives. Think of anything bad that might have happened in your life – losing a job, being bullied, losing your voice, not standing up for yourself, being hurt or hurting another. At the time, you thought you'd never survive what happened. You felt terrible and you thought you would always feel that way. Now, with distance and perspective, often you can see that you survived and perhaps did much more than that; sometimes you can see how the experience might have been a catalyst for wonderful changes. If you can't do that, if you still live with anger, sorrow, pain, guilt or shame, then if you want to be happier and healthier, it's definitely time to change your story.

## LIVING YOUR LIFE BACKWARDS

Martha Beck, one of my favourite authors, talks about living your life backwards, where you tell your story from the end to the beginning. You start by finding something that's really good in your life now and work back from there. Then you think about what happened to get you to that good thing or great person, home or job. What was the thing that immediately preceded it? And before that? She suggests going back in a series of steps so you understand the different events, choices and people that led you to that point. For instance, if my favourite thing is the house I currently live in, I could go back to the house I lived in previously but was too small for four teenagers although I was very happy there, then to a house that was too small for a family but was all I could afford as a single parent, then back to a house that I jointly owned outright and where there were lots of savings in the bank – a house that many people envied – but where I had been extremely unhappy. When I left that house it disrupted many things and people, but it led to a place where I could be real, raise happier children and find a place I could really call home. Martha says people who take the time to do this become 'Stargazers', as you look at life from the opposite end of a telescope. In so doing, you choose to see that your destiny is to have what she calls your favourite thing in the end – not the bad luck or bad thing that began that journey.

Writer Byron Katie argues that even though we can only live in the present, people still spend their time focused on changing the past. What a waste of energy, as nothing you do can change it one little bit – not thinking, not therapy, not crying, not screaming, not prayer, not talking about it, not ignoring it. And to continue to live in the past is to continue to live with pain and not to enjoy the present.

## OUR 'I AMS'

Our stories are important to us because they are our 'I ams'; they are how we define ourselves at the deepest level. The 'I am' you choose to use will empower you or limit you, move you forwards, or keep you trapped in the past, as powerless as a victim.

What better tool is there than journalling to help you choose to tell your story from a different perspective than you have used to date? Why not take the time to be honest with yourself? Have you thought about the stories you've been telling about yourself lately? Do they still fit with who you are now? Are they the truth – the whole truth? Would an interested and compassionate observer point out that you hadn't got elements of it quite right (or entirely wrong)? Is it time instead to redefine yourself powerfully, shake off what no longer fits, cast away the burdens you have carried for so long and find out who you are now?

## REWRITE YOUR STORY

Could you rewrite your story in a different way instead of the one you keep telling yourself and others (the one that stops you stepping into your light, trusting others, loving again, going for that dream job)? Could you tell it in a different way, so it's a love story, a ghost story, a mystery, a poem? Could you find a more positive way to tell it, one that knows there is no failure, only feedback? Could you just write out your old story one final time and burn it in a ritual, knowing it's time to *let go* right now? If it's a really negative story, Byron Katie suggests if you can give someone a peaceful reason to hold onto it, then keep it. I love the phrase 'a peaceful reason to hold onto it' and it's actually helped me to let a lot of stories go.

There are always alternative versions of a story depending on who writes it or who listens to it. Freedom fighting is called terrorism by others who do not see their freedom challenged. Some called Nelson Mandela a freedom fighter; others called him a terrorist and do not appreciate the fact he became a world statesman. Nelson Mandela could have been defined by the title of freedom fighter or by the bitterness engendered by twenty-five years in prison. Instead of choosing bitterness and revenge as his story, focusing on injustice or his anger and loss, he decided to focus on what he had learned about changing human hearts. He realized you can't do that with violence and he chose to change his story to one where his own heart was changed and he was willing to see through different eyes, cooperate with others, forgive those who had wronged him and embrace those with opposing political views. Many who have gone through very similar experiences have not done the same; they chose a different story. Who made the most difference?

## CHOOSE THE STORY YOU WANT TO TELL NOW

Behind the stories that bind us to our past lies fear and this is not the way for you to live. It's time to grab your courage in both hands and live your life well. Accept what is; we cannot change what has happened in our past, but we can change the emotions, our perspective, what we focus on. Now is all that matters, and there is no fear in the present moment; try it and see.

Choose the story you want to tell from now on, using your journal to work through what you need to. Seek outside help if you know that is what you need (this is a sign of great strength and wisdom where it is used as necessary). We never serve the world or those we love by living in the shadow of the past or the shadows others chose for us in the past. Trust me; you will find a way to be, a new way, but one that does not start and end with fear. Our happiness is our responsibility; this is the greatest lesson anyone can learn – and though it might start with where we came from, we get to choose the ending. And that starts with the stories we tell ourselves about who we are, what we are capable of – and what happens next.

# Change your story, change your life

1 How did you end up being where you are now? What is your story?

2 When you tell your story to others, what significant parts do you leave out?

3 If you told your story from the other person's point of view, what changes?

4 Do you see patterns in your life?

5 What from your past still holds you back from creating the future you want?

6 If you are honest, do you keep blaming other people for the way your life has turned out?

7 Have other people with a similar story been able to move forwards?

8 Where have you been strong in your life? Where have you been resourceful?

9 What are you thankful for in your life now, that you wouldn't have, because of something that was less than totally positive at the time?

10 What lessons have you learned through failure, hurt, rejection, shame, guilt, anger?

11 Who could support you in letting go of something you've held onto for too long (including resentment)?

**12** If your life story had a theme, what might that be? Does that theme recall something you were once told about yourself? Was that true?

**13** What part of your story are you avoiding so you don't have to handle the emotions attached?

**14** What story do you want to tell about yourself going forwards that is positive?

**15** What do you have to change to tell this story authentically?

## Choose a thought to concentrate on from the choices below:

I create my own life story, I can create a new story.

I am powerful, I am enough.

'The worst loneliness is not to be comfortable with yourself.'

*Mark Twain*

## 16 Strengthen your self-esteem

### The meaning of self-esteem

For many years, self-esteem was the Holy Grail of self-help, so let me say at the outset what self-esteem means to me. In 2009, I went to a conference run by the Centre for Confidence in Glasgow on how the obsession with self-esteem was a ticking time bomb in the UK, as the results had already become apparent in America. What we had done by teaching our children to believe in themselves and to be confident was to fail to teach them responsibility, and how to accept feedback and failure. Consequently, they had grown up to be arrogant, unable to bounce back because they never had the chance to build up resilience. This wasn't new — the Joseph Rowntree Foundation published a report in 2001 that said the same thing.

## BE REALISTIC

I am talking about a realistic self-esteem that is aware of weaknesses as well as strengths. Or am I? When I ran staff appraisals, very occasionally people would recognize no weaknesses and accept no feedback; those are hard people to manage! Much more often, when I asked for examples of weaknesses so we could work on them or around them, I would be given a long list – but when I asked for a list of strengths, I would be met with stammers or silence. Sometimes I would send people off with the 'homework' assignment of finding ten strengths, as it is only when people know their strengths that they will be really effective in their jobs. Healthy self-esteem is a realistic confidence in your abilities that gives you confidence to take risks in other areas. Low self-esteem is driven by fear of failure or rejection and it manifests itself everywhere, meaning people may live a shadow half-life which does not serve them or their world.

## WHY EVEN BOTHER?

We do need to work on our self-esteem, because it's important to us as individuals and it is important to our family members, partners, other relationships (including work and social) and to the part we play as members of society. Research shows that those with very low or very high self-esteem are more likely to be involved in crime and violence, to have addiction issues or exhibit other self-destructive behaviours. In the workplace, those with self-esteem issues are less likely to make independent decisions, take risks or act on their own initiative; alternatively, they are too ready to do that and take risks that are extreme or unnecessary. Low self-esteem can lead to anxiety and depression, staying in work that is low-paid or brings you no joy; it can lead to difficulties in forming positive relationships, both in and outside of work.

The key time to build self-esteem is in a child's early life, first by the adults who are most important to them, and then by teachers. They (and everyone else from neighbours, friends and other people in their wider world) will play a part in this – so if you were lucky, you had a great start in life. If those who were teaching you also struggled with self-esteem issues, or otherwise limited your ability to see yourself in this way, then there is no doubt your experience may have been painful and is likely to have had a long-term impact. Bullying, criticism, abuse, a lack of love or making you feel that you need to be quiet and/or perfect all the time may have driven you to hide or constantly seek success and validation elsewhere. Now this is simply part of your past and can't be changed – but you *can* change. Understanding the 'why' is only ever the first part of change (and sometimes you don't even need to know why, you just need to want to change).

## THE BUCK STOPS WITH YOU

From this point on, you can't blame anyone else, because you know now that you create your own reality. That starts now, not in the future (when you might feel better, when you get that new car, partner, house, job, etc.). You can change the emotions attached to these memories and you can change what you believe about yourself – and both these internal changes will lead to great external changes. Eleanor Roosevelt said no one can make you feel inferior without your permission; she knew self-esteem was an inside job. I'm still a work in progress but it is getting better all the time. When I started, because I was learning new skills and a new way of being, I went from a quiet mouse who didn't stand up for herself in many situations to a lion who roared at everyone – and I didn't much like either of those people. Finding a balance somewhere in between is a much happier place for me, because it's real.

Remember that just because you are telling yourself that you are worthless, incapable of doing things or improving yourself, or that you can't change doesn't make these statements true! Stream of consciousness writing (*see page 20*) or answering specific questions in your journal can really help you see what you're thinking/remembering/worrying about, so you can start to challenge and change it. You will also start to see what it is that you really need (emotionally and practically) – like putting better boundaries in place, better self-care, being more assertive, learning to manage your money or time better, or deciding to end a particular relationship. You can see what you are waiting for to make you feel better (like getting an apology, being braver or thinner, winning the lottery, or for someone else to do this for you) – and see that you need to stop waiting and start taking action. You are your own alchemist, so why wait for a better time than to change than *now*?

# Strengthen your self-esteem

1 What core beliefs do you have about yourself? Fill in ten answers to 'I believe I am _____'.

2 Would you say what you say to yourself to a good friend who was similar?

3 How do you practise self-care for yourself? How do you see others practising self-care?

**4** Where do you fail to assert yourself?

**5** How can you start to practise standing up for yourself?

## And:

Draw a vertical line down a spare piece of paper, or a page in a blank journal; on the left-hand side, write down the comments you hear most often in your head/that you say to yourself, and on the right-hand side, find a positive way to reframe those or find evidence that they are not always true (or true at all).

Start recording one thing each day that makes you feel good or where you were, or are, a success.

Create an emergency list of ten or twenty things you like about yourself and keep it at the back of your journal if you need a quick reminder on a bad day.

## Choose a thought to concentrate on and make choices from:

When I respect myself, other people respect me too.

I do better as I know better.

# 17 *Widen your comfort zone*

'Do one thing
every day that
scares you.'
*Eleanor Roosevelt*

### It's time to fly

I love butterflies. For me, they are the symbol of change, hope
and freedom. I use them in cards I make for people, combining
them with words, pictures and colours that I feel are important.
A caterpillar goes through a process that is not yet fully understood
to transform into a butterfly. We don't actually know if a butterfly
believes the silence of the pupae stage is the end of the world, but
from the outside in, it could look like that. What they go through
to change is an extreme transformation; the death of one life to live
another. Some people are who they are now because of this type
of experience, ending one thing to become another, consciously or
unconsciously, willingly or unwillingly. Most of us don't go through
such a radical change – our process takes longer and the only
butterflies we know are those in our stomach.

## YOU NEVER STAY STILL – BUT DON'T GO ROUND IN CIRCLES

Change is inevitable; it's part of life. You never stay still, and neither does the life around you. We must all be willing to take risks if we are to live the life we want. Too often we imprison ourselves with our fears of 'what ifs', what people might say, failure, rejection and hurt. When we are the gatekeepers who stop life entering, we also halt our soul's freedom.

Start listening to what the universe is whispering to your soul and dare to be happier by having the courage to take that first small step to your freedom. Is that too much to consider? Do you believe that change is always hard, always painful and always means the death of something? When you view change like that, it will be like that, so find a better way to think about it.

## LEAVE YOUR COMFORT ZONE

Let me make this clear: you will never live the life you want to live if you don't try to widen that comfort zone. It's like being in a prison of your own making. A choice to leave the place where things are familiar would mean you are taking a risk – but with just a few short steps, you could be out.

So what stories are you telling yourself that are keeping you where you are? Why do you think living in that way is safer than stepping out into the world and daring to be uniquely you? Will your life really be poorer for deciding to follow your own heart and dreams instead of what someone else suggests for you? Will you really find that any failure kills you stone dead or that you can't rise from the ashes like a phoenix? If you think like that, you're reading the wrong stories; you can choose to read different stories and create a different life. And that starts right now.

## CONSCIOUSLY CHOOSE CHANGE

On the basis that all change starts somewhere, why not choose to be in control of the change, where possible? There will always be times when external events stop you in your tracks. These might involve a major loss that needs time to address (not to heal so much as to learn a different way of being that honours that loss but allows you to still live a good life). Sometimes these events might teach us that we are much more courageous and capable than we ever thought.

Outside of these extraordinary experiences, we have so much more control over change than we sometimes think; we can consciously decide to be in control of the change and take action to respond to it or deal with it. Surely that is a much better option than having our lives changed by default or by our passivity (as if we constantly had to live at the whim of the fates). Remember, the change doesn't have to be big; I advocate and encourage small changes, to widen the comfort zone slowly until you get used to change and begin to trust yourself again. So it may start with little steps (like changing how we think or changing one thing we do) – but all journeys begin with that first step. We can then choose to see setbacks as the end of the road, or as temporary obstacles to find ways around or help us change direction, if needs be. It's only by daring to take that first step that we ever change our landscape. Take the risk, learn from the experience – and learn to flourish.

## DEVELOP YOUR ACTION PLAN

Use your journal to develop an action plan and to capture feedback. You can use a technique like clustering to help you build new dreams or rework older ones. Clustering ensures that what we write down around a theme is done quickly, allowing your unconscious mind to help you along. Think of the one thing you want to try or explore and put it in the centre of the page. Breathe deeply three times and ask that all that is necessary will be brought to your mind, and then just start writing fast.

Your dream will start to take shape depending on the questions you ask. So do it several times with different questions. You could ask, 'Who will I need to help me achieve this?'. Or you might ask, 'What exactly is it I want to share with the world?' to help you clarify the message, and 'How could I do this?' or 'What do I need to do next?' to come up with practical ideas.

Once a cluster page is complete, you can use it to build an action plan, breaking it down into appropriate steps. Then you could make a to-do list of what you will do today/this week/this month. Having this in place will always keep you moving forward, particularly when you decide to do three or five things a day from your list of goals and actions. Your world won't change until you take steps to make it change (and you never know where one step towards a goal will take you). Of course, hindsight might show where you made mistakes, but you can't live life right now with that perspective; all you can do is take the best next step you can – and learn from it! Once you start taking small steps, you will find that your wisdom and confidence grow, allowing you to take bigger steps.

Sometimes instead of action plans, the risk starts with changing your thoughts. If you find that you have limiting beliefs, change them to enabling beliefs, or challenge them by finding examples when that belief wasn't true. When you can't change a situation, all you can do is change your thoughts; this is what Victor Frankl said was the 'last of the human freedoms'. Change your thoughts and focus by changing who you spend time with, what you read, what you watch, which seminars or workshops you attend. Allow this to stretch, challenge and feed you.

## FEAR ITSELF IS NOT THE ISSUE

Learn lessons quickly, and as you change and grow, you will find other lessons are easier as a result. Nearly everyone feels fearful when faced with something new, but if nearly everyone feels fearful, and if some people actually make changes, then the fear itself is not the issue. It's the failure to take action that's the issue!

Step out, and stretch yourself; like an elastic band, you will find you can't go back to exactly the same place you started from. Your world has stretched, and as you've grown, the new world becomes comfortable until that is your new comfort zone. We can enlarge our comfort zones to whatever size we want, like blowing up a balloon. Sometimes you will take one big, long breath, but mostly, it will just be a few little breaths at a time, slowly expanding the boundaries, and soon that balloon is flying high. As Ralph Waldo Emerson said, 'What we fear doing most is usually what we most need to do.' Do it!

# Widen your comfort zone

1 What is failing to change costing you?

2 What old identities, roles or labels would it be helpful to let go of?

3 What will you lose, and what will you gain, by moving out of your comfort zone?

4 Can you accept that it may take time to become comfortable again?

5 How might your sense of who you are change by widening your comfort zone?

6 What could you surrender to or embrace rather than fight against?

7 What parts of yourself can you bring with you, and what parts is it time to let go of?

8 What new habits and routines can you develop or will you develop?

9 What strengths do you have now that will help you cope with any change?

**10** Who can support you in what you want to change or do?

**11** What beliefs do you have about the change that might prevent you from taking action?

**12** What is ending as something else is beginning? How can you honour that transition?

**13** What values, dreams and priorities are you not expressing by living as you do now?

## Choose a thought to concentrate on from the choices below:

The only limits I have are the ones I set for myself. Today, I choose growth.

I let go of my unwillingness to trust myself. I will cope, and cope well – for I've coped well enough so far.

'Fear defeats more people than any other one thing in the world.'

*Ralph Waldo Emerson*

# 18 Live a fearless life

**We're all frightened of something; don't let it be life**

Living a fearless life takes courage, obviously. Everyone is frightened of something — flying, dying, wasps, spiders, rats or mice, snakes, public speaking, family, neighbours or neighbourhood crime, being alone, being left on the shelf, beginnings, endings, cotton wool or even shiny buttons. Yes, I really knew someone who was very frightened of shiny buttons — but had the courage to admit to that. Some fears turn into phobias, instinctive reactions where our responses involve no thought because the fear is buried so deep in our unconscious mind it becomes automatic (although this can be quickly changed by an NLP tool called Fast Phobia Cure). Our fears protect us in some ways, so we physically and wisely move away from wasps or snakes, for instance — but more often, they imprison us. When we let our fears, or our worries about what others might say or what might happen take over, or we fear failure or rejection, it can severely limit our lives. We choose fear by how we think, and by what we do — and don't do.

## IMPRISONED BY WORDS

We also imprison ourselves by the words we use. We say we must, we could, we can't, we should, all of which are possibilities for the future and driven by necessity rather than a desire to just do what we want to do. More often than not, those words of necessity could be changed – or should be challenged. If you change 'I can't' to 'I won't', 'I should' to 'I choose not to', then you can sometimes see the honesty that lies behind your failure to follow your dreams or take that first step to change or stand up for your life. What stops you daring to be who you are? What stops you daring to be happier, free, courageous, or present? Only you can answer those questions.

## IMPRISONED BY LABELS

We imprison ourselves by the labels others give us, where we choose to accept them, or by the labels we give ourselves. I'm sure you've heard people say they are 'just a housewife', 'just a cleaner', 'a black woman', 'a gay partner', 'a widow', 'unemployed', 'elderly', 'fat and ugly', 'an angry man' or 'a lonely heart'. And with a label comes the appropriate box, so people become boxed in by their beliefs about what that word means to them and others, and the box becomes familiar and because they know they can handle what they know, they keep the label and close the lid.

## IMPRISONED BY OUR 'BE CAREFULS'

We are told to 'be careful' from our earliest days, when we live in a world of fairy stories, monsters, ghosts and giants. Our mothers or other carers warn us to be careful, not to do that, stay there, stop. Parents often project their own fears onto us as they try to protect themselves as well as their children. Perhaps we choose our parents so we learn the lessons our soul and spirit need to learn, even if we feel criticized, judged and anxious as we get older and follow our chosen path. Yet you are never your parents. You are not their views, opinions or personalities. You are YOU – warts, mistakes and faults, as well as gifts, skills and beauty.

## FINDING FREEDOM

We have to find our own path and walk it, with people who will walk alongside us to support and love us. Walking our own path is freedom! It may mean that along the way we leave some people behind as we walk much more quickly than they are prepared to, or if we follow a different route to the one they wanted to take. We must learn to respect and honour their right to walk their own paths, face their own fears, become their own heroes (who can fight monsters and giants) and learn their own soul lessons. Growing up, we lived in a world of 'be carefuls' and the world was a dangerous place, if you chose to see it like that. We are taught early to be careful, which often just reminds us that you can't control life and you might get hurt. Parents do more than just protect us if this is excessive; they pass on their own lack of belief in themselves to us. My brother chose to see life as an adventure, running an outdoor survival school and activity centre, and says his motivation for getting out there and *trying* was because he was so often told not to when he was a child.

In her book *Feel the Fear and Do It Anyway,* Susan Jeffers told us there were different levels of fear: surface level (obvious ones that happen because we are human), states of mind (the ones we create ourselves by our thinking), and ultimately, the fear that we can't handle whatever happens. That is the ultimate fear – and it can be paralyzing.

## WHY AM I AFRAID?

Sometimes we might not know where a fear came from. At times like this, you don't need to know, just accept that change is needed and decide to do it. Even if you can't control anything else in the outside world, you can choose to control your thinking and fears, because that's an inside job. Look at what fears lie behind you remaining a victim, think about the benefits you will gain from behaving like this, but also what it costs you. What are you not doing by waiting for the fear to go? Be really honest; look at all the things you're afraid of. What are the excuses that are stopping you from doing something and what might be genuine reasons? What could you deal with alone, or deal with if someone supported you? What ways have you already found of getting around it, by a variety of coping strategies?

The only way to get rid of fear is to face it head-on. Trust me. When you decide to do this, you will immediately feel better about yourself. Susan Jeffers said that we wrongly interpret fear as a signal to retreat, when instead if we pushed through the fear, we would stop feeling helpless. I have found this to be true.

## JUST DO IT!

Fear is either an anchor to hold us where we are, or a sail to help us move into new waters. There are plenty of people out there doing what you are not doing because of fear – and being successful or happier. So fear is never the problem, it is how we freeze-frame our life with it, rather than create, or allow in, success or happiness. Start telling yourself that you *can* handle things. Begin by changing your language. Look at what you've written and rewrite what's there by using power words rather than pain words, words that create the possibility of change or optimism. Even just changing 'It's not my fault' to 'I accept responsibility for my part in…', or 'I can't' to 'I can't yet' can change how you think.

And then, just do it – do it scared, if needs be. As the British biologist and anthropologist Thomas Huxley said, 'Make up your mind to act decidedly and take the consequences. No good is ever done in this world by hesitation.' The day you decide to do something instead of accepting your imagined fears as all being true, the day you decide to stop avoiding what makes you fearful or stop spending time hoping and wishing the fears will go away, is the day your life changes. If you took an inventory of all the times you've faced fears, broken through fear or dragged yourself through to the other side of fear, you would be amazed. It's just that you easily forget them! Step out. As Susan Jeffers says – feel the fear and do it anyway. You are always stronger than you think, and you WILL handle what life brings you.

# Live a fearless life

**1** What are you afraid of?

**2** What labels do you routinely use that might keep you fearful?

**3** How has fear stopped you living the life you really want?

**4** What does living a fearless life look like to you?

**5** Are your fears rational? Do you have a reason to think like this or could this be someone else's belief that doesn't belong to you anymore?

**6** Do your fears keep you safe? Safe enough, or *too* safe?

**7** If you were to let go of your fear, what great things could happen?

**8** What's the worst thing that could happen?

**9** What could your fear be teaching you?

**10** Who can help you get where you want to be?

**11** Will it be worse to fail or never attempt it in the first place?

**12** Will you regret not going for what you want to?

**13** Where have you pushed through fear to do something you want to do before now?

**14** What do you need to give yourself permission to do?

## And:

Have a conversation with your fear. Write a letter to your fear or write as if you are speaking to your fears, and then allow your fear to speak to you.

Write ten answers to 'It's now OK to _____'.

## Choose a thought to concentrate on from the choices below:

I can find calmness and the strength to feel fear and still do things scared.

I will lean into what I fear, knowing there is no failure, only feedback.

# 19 Make stronger connections

'I am part of all
that I have met.'
*Alfred, Lord Tennyson*

## Real connection matters

We are now connected in a way undreamed of before, to people all around the world, through phones, emails, webcams and social media. My life is richer for it, through new friends and information, and because it enables me to keep in touch with family as they choose to follow their dreams. But if we are not careful, this connectedness in space can become the norm and we fail to connect with those we spend time breathing the same air.

A man was interviewed on BBC Breakfast News one morning and he said that he used various social media outlets to keep up with his friends. The interviewer was baffled, wondering why he didn't just pick up the phone or arrange to meet them for a coffee or a drink, and the man couldn't really answer except to say that he preferred the 'Facebook method'. But as only 7 per cent of what we actually say using words counts towards the overall message, if he did actually meet up with people, he might receive an entirely different message and a whole different level of connection.

## NO ONE IS AN ISLAND

Though some people deliberately choose to live in isolation and contemplation, they are a small minority. Most of us not only need to connect with others, we long for deeper connections. When we fail to connect with those around us, we lose a fundamental part of who we are. When we don't spend time with people and invest in them, it is very easy to become lonely; loneliness has now been shown to be as bad for your physical health and longevity as it is for your mental health.

As we move towards increasing levels of automation and artificial intelligence, we could find ourselves with a smaller and smaller group of people to talk to. Yet we all need something living to connect with, even if that is just our pet, because we simply weren't made to be self-contained, living as individual 'islands'. Experiments in the USA by Dr René Spitz in the 1940s showed that this is a need we have as soon as we are born. A group of babies were divided into two institutions. The first group were kept in an orphanage and looked after by a nurse. The second group were allowed to be cared for by their mothers – who happened to be in prison. All were fed and changed as often as they needed to be, but the studies showed that this difference really affected child development – it was the connections that mattered.

## FRIENDSHIPS MATTER

Are you surrounded by acquaintances but long for deeper friendships, or do you struggle to make new friends because you are introverted or have beliefs about friendship, trust or your own self-worth? If you have been waiting for your friends to call you, to ask you out for a meal, then remember that the old adage still rings true: 'to have a friend, you need to be a friend'. At its basic level, friendship sits in the middle of psychologist Abraham Maslow's Hierarchy of Needs. After our physiological and safety needs are met, we should have enough energy free to develop emotionally based relationships that matter. This is about being accepted, being heard, and it is also about integrity, trust, loyalty and fun. If you fulfil someone's needs, they will want to deepen that relationship with you – if they believe you are genuine.

## WHAT ARE YOUR RELATIONSHIP NEEDS?

What is important to you in social relationships? If you could design a new friend, what would they look like? Where are you likely to meet such a friend? It is unlikely you will meet one sitting in your house, so this will require action. Brainstorm ideas, put down as many as you can think off, no matter how far-fetched, and then evaluate them later. Choose the top four or five that feel right to you – and then take action!

Write down your action plan and put in dates for which you aim to achieve each one. Remember to celebrate your successes.

Friends or partners are not meant to be clones. By this, I mean that they may well have much in common with you – but they will not agree on every view you have or be interested in everything that makes you tick. Learn to speak your truth while respecting differences in opinions and tastes. Don't correct them or continually argue with them, unless it is crucial – and even then, don't do it in front of others. The ego is a fragile thing, as we all want to feel good about ourselves. Decide where you must take a stand to avoid compromising yourself – but if you have to choose between being right or caring, always choose caring.

## LISTENING MATTERS MORE THAN TALKING

One of the hardest things to learn is to listen properly. You have two ears and one mouth for a reason. As someone is talking to you, don't think about what you are going to say next. Instead, carefully consider what they are saying, really focus on it, and try to understand where they are coming from. Reflective listening is a skill anyone can learn – it simply means that you listen carefully and then reflect back to that person what they have said to you – for example, 'So you feel that when X happened, you believed Y was inevitable'.

## FRIENDSHIPS NEED WORK

There are times when you meet someone and you know from the start that they are a kindred spirit. Then there will be instances when the connection grows over time as you get to know someone better. There will also be relationships that surprise you, where you end up connecting at a deeper level with someone you never would have expected. After that, friendship does require some work and commitment – after all, *someone* has to pick up the phone, send that text, pop in, email or arrange a catch-up, don't they? Life has a habit of getting in the way so you feel overwhelmed by just living, working and keeping body and soul together.

We fool ourselves into thinking we can concentrate on friendships when 'things get easier'. Time is such a precious commodity; you only have so much and it is up to you how you use it. Choose to slump down in front of a TV – or arrange to meet someone to catch up, have fun together and build some sort of memory! Take time to build stronger, deeper relationships by being vulnerable enough to reveal yourself to others. Invest most of your time in friends who support you as you support them, and who aren't afraid to ask the hard questions when they need asking. Relationships need to be nurtured or they will die.

## MAKING NEW FRIENDS

When making friends, it's always worth persevering for a while – but not for too long. Sometimes you will find that friendships are hard to make because of other people's ideas or assumptions. No matter how hard you try to be part of a particular crowd or to get them to accept you, it just doesn't happen. I don't think being connected should require that much energy; it will be pretty natural when you are trying to connect with people who are of a similar mind or have similar values to you.

If you aren't making friends, start by deciding what your type of friend 'looks like' and then set the intention of meeting them. Take assertiveness classes, or watch videos and read books about how to assert yourself; then put it into practice. Start being interested in people – more interested in them than you are in yourself. Perhaps you don't make friends because you are 'too shy', 'too old', 'too fat', 'too grumpy', 'too thin' or 'too set in your ways'. Or perhaps these are barriers you are putting up that are simply excuses. Feel the fear (of rejection, ridicule or vulnerability) and do it anyway – it is worth the risk, it is worth the investment.

## CONNECT WITH FAMILY

This is where the connection with others starts. Family is usually your first experience of what is called 'other than me', where your ego begins to understand that, actually, you aren't the centre of the universe. Most families aren't perfect because they are made up of human beings; some are unsafe places to be, where children or partners are isolated, ignored, sidelined, or have to cope with hugely complex issues or fractured lives, drink or drug addiction or even physical or mental abuse. To have been part of a home where a parent or parents loved you and wanted only the best for you is a great blessing that isn't shared by everyone – but your birth family doesn't have to be the only family you have. As an adult, you can choose to create a group that nurtures and keeps you safe, that treats you with respect and dignity.

## CONNECTIONS AS YOU GROW

As a child, if you are lucky, you will make some good connections outside your family. Children make them easily; there is innocence at this stage when they believe everyone is their friend. They just connect, they don't need to think about it or analyze it. There is often a special relationship between older people and small children, possibly because they have more time and patience, because neither party fears rejection, or because both parties know 'who they are', so there are no barriers. Or it could be that they just place a high value on their ability to connect because they realize that in the end what matters are relationships. After that, connections can become harder. When you go to school you will be popular, unpopular or somewhere in between. You begin to understand that there are rules that govern behaviour. Speak when you are spoken to, stand up/sit down, take your break and now play. There are routines at school and then routines at home or at the after-school club or the childminder's. Activities fill up the day, before you spend time watching TV or on the internet, all of which often leave no time to strengthen connections and build new ones.

## CONNECT WITH YOUR COLLEAGUES

Studies have shown that you need to have a 'best friend' at work to make it a happy place, someone you can talk to in confidence, moan to, spend time with – and when you have a best friend, you'll be less stressed. You spend time with work colleagues because you have to – and some you would never choose to socialize with, but you can still connect with them, because you will learn from all of them. Each has their own world map, their own experience, ways of doing things, and even if you learn from the negative experiences (as in what you won't do), you will still have learned. More often than not though, you can make strong connections at work while you are there. The connections may not mean that the relationship or even friendship is maintained once you leave, but they will still be there while you work, and will make your working life easier, and some friendships may last long after you leave.

## CONNECT WITH YOUR COMMUNITY – AND THE WIDER WORLD

No matter where you are in the world, you always have a world of your own. When you find a job, you will become part of that particular community, and when you move into a flat or house, you will be part of that community. And beyond that is the wider neighbourhood and then the community of the world. In the same way you could choose to shut yourself off and stay in your room, so you can choose to ignore these wider communities. That doesn't mean they go away. If you aren't sure how to get involved in your community, start asking questions and you will find that once you start looking, you will be spoilt for choice. Start small, at your local level and who knows where in the world it might lead you.

## FINALLY, CONNECT WITH YOURSELF

Of all the connections you need to make, this is most important one! Did it surprise you that this was included in the list of connections? We can easily become disconnected from ourselves, from our dreams and from the longings of our hearts. You will find that your journal is a vital tool to help you connect or reconnect with yourself and your feelings, emotions, values, beliefs and dreams. This is the one relationship that ultimately matters; it will guide you in all the other connections you make, or decide not to make. Strength comes through reflection; you have to stop what you are doing to see what you were doing; strange, but true. And as you start to slow down, it helps you become more focused on what really matters.

## IN CONCLUSION

The power of relationships is in our connections. People in our lives can be neutral, drains or radiators. They can drain the energy from us or radiate their own energy so we benefit from it. Look at who you connect with, see how many rob you of energy and start to disconnect from them. Choose to surround yourself with positive people who inspire, nurture and encourage you. Our connections with people who share our passions, motivate us to greatness, who keep us persevering when we feel like giving up are the ones that change us for the better.

Whatever connections you make you will learn from – the differences as well as the similarities. If we were all the same, how boring our lives would be! We need to experience, to connect at the deepest level to grow into who we are meant to be, to remember that we are not unconnected islands and to connect to such an extent that we know what someone's heart might be longing for, or in need of.

# Make stronger connections

1  What assumptions have you made instead of asking direct questions?

2  When communication has broken down, has it been a battle of wills or values?

3  Are there times when you could spend more energy on seeing another person's viewpoint? Could your viewpoint be redefined?

4  Are you acting authentically, so what you say and do is congruent?

**5** Do you ever listen to what isn't being said?

**6** In which circumstances are you failing to connect with the people who really matter to you?

**7** What beliefs might you be using as an excuse not to connect more deeply?

**8** What can you do to connect more deeply with others?

**9** Who can you reach out to, to build a better relationship?

**10** What are your relationship needs?

**11** Are some of your current friends emotional vampires who don't support you?

**12** How can you let them go to allow space for people who will support you?

## And, on a sheet of paper or in a blank journal:
Write ten answers to 'What is important to me in social relationships?'

Design a new friend. What do you do together? How do you treat and support each other?

## Choose a thought to concentrate on and make choices from:

I love and accept others, just as they love and accept me.

Today, I choose to take time to connect deeply with people.

'You don't love someone for their looks, or their clothes, or for their fancy car, but because they sing a song only you can hear.'

*Oscar Wilde*

# 20 *Improve romantic relationships*

### The fairy story

When we find a relationship with someone special we *know* that when we fall in love it will be forever. It happened for Cinderella and Snow White after all! Snow White was my favourite childhood story and I was sure that I would 'find my prince and live happily ever after', but real life can step in and people move on. The connection at a deep level is no longer there; one partner doesn't keep up with changes in the other or what matters to them isn't being satisfied in the busy-ness of life, or someone else becomes more important. When this happens the love and romance you felt at first gets caught in the crossfire and dies.

### Breaking up is hard to do

Breakups are rarely easy. If I had my time again (no regrets, remember, as the lessons our soul needs are learned), I would have made my breakups a lot easier on everyone concerned. I know now (with the insight of hindsight) that the collateral damage would have been significantly limited, had I taken time out to reflect or think things through, or see them from a different point of view. I didn't know then what Lepore and Greenberg had discovered – that journalling is a really useful tool for those going through a relationship breakup.[13] We don't go into a love relationship expecting it to die, but if that happens, then journalling can also help you work out why it ended.[14] With that knowledge, sometimes the relationship can be saved, where both partners are willing to change; at other times, at least it helps you not to make the same mistakes again.

I know journalling would have helped me sort so many things out more quickly, helped me move towards love again with a better understanding of who I was and make better choices based on my current values. Instead, because my identity was wrapped up in the relationships I chose in the vacuum – as a focus for finding my own self-worth or just 'wanting to be loved' – they often ended traumatically. When my first marriage ended, it involved an entirely fresh start for me (house, job and friends). I was convinced that I would never find love again.

## STARTING OVER

And yet I *did* find love; I found it after I read Cheryl Richardson's book *Stand Up for Your Life* and diligently did the work she demanded with her questions. I put better boundaries in place, I stood up for myself more, I began to see my worth not based on other's opinions, I started (even then) to dare to be happier. And that led to a deeper, stronger love, one that I'm still thankful for every single day. That is mostly the measure of the man I fell in love with – who was willing to take on four teenage children and whose wedding vows said:

'I look forward to spending the rest of my life with you and our children, sharing the good times, supporting you through the bad. I offer myself to you as a partner in life, and to our children as a parent, accepting the responsibility of being a loving and guiding parent to them. From this day forward, I make this solemn vow, that I will always be there for you and our children, in sickness and in heath, for richer or poorer, till death do us part.'

As he named each of the children individually, there wasn't a dry eye in the house. I remember this wave of emotion sweeping the room behind us; a physical energy we could feel. However, our happy marriage isn't just down to these words or that commitment, and it isn't down to luck either. Romance is important and that often comes down to small, everyday gestures rather than big statements, because this is what shows a commitment to love every day.

## ROMANCE IS ALSO REAL LIFE

We've both worked at different things during the course of our marriage. I've found journalling to be a huge help to me in sorting my emotions out, letting go of my baggage so I don't keep bringing that into my current relationship and in learning to love myself and becoming whole. You don't find the other half; you find another whole person.

Journalling allows us to express difficult thoughts or feelings we may otherwise keep inside. If you keep things inside long enough it has an effect on both your mental and physical health. In my first marriage, for the last two years, I was sick and tired every three weeks, taking to my bed – I can now see this was because I was sick and tired of what my marriage had become at that point. If I had written my feelings down, my negative moods would have lifted, I wouldn't have become ill and I would have been able to address the issues more clearly.

## THE PART IN-BETWEEN

So we know journalling works for breakups and endings – but what about the part in-between? Can it help us to have a loving, healthy, open relationship? Yes. Journalling has allowed me to be more intimate, honest and receptive to love. It's allowed me to work things out that had nothing to do to with him but were still baggage from my past that I was putting onto him or that was affecting us. It has helped me recognize the times I get angry with him when I've no need to do that, or when I'm blowing things out of proportion, or when there are things that we need to talk about openly but I've been avoiding by saying 'nothing' is wrong and I was 'fine'. Sometimes, that can be something as small as noticing the words I'm choosing when I'm writing about him. If I review what I've written and find mainly negative, hard words, then I quickly realize I'm focusing only on his negative traits and forgetting that these are hugely outweighed by his positive ones. Journalling helps me to take a balanced, realistic view of our relationship.

The main way it helps me to ensure the depth of our relationship is by preventing me from suppressing my emotions. I was brought up to be quiet and I learned very early on that it was better not to say how I felt, but to keep things calm and put on a front. I lived with many masks – and am grateful that the breakup of my first marriage gave me the courage to take them off. Suppressing or avoiding emotions is never good: they just go somewhere else and affect your health – and you often become a victim or martyr, unable to see options or find coping strategies. When you journal, you can't avoid things – they come up, and once they have your attention, you have to do something about them by finding ways to understand them and then sorting them out. (If you don't do the work here, these will keep rising to the surface to remind you anyway.) Focusing on the positives, working through the emotions or taking action to resolve things or move on, and writing about things that may be too hard to say face to face, can help to reframe an experience, remind you to seek outside help or support if needed.

## SPEAK UP WHEN YOU NEED TO

We frequently censor ourselves from saying what it is that we truly want to say – and often this is wise, as once said, things can't be unsaid. However, we may have many reasons for not speaking our truth, even in our most intimate relationships, but most of them are unhelpful – like fear of rejection/criticism, of hurting someone's feelings, self-doubt/feelings of inferiority, lack of confidence or habits of silence that we've developed over time. Our angry words and seething rage do the same harm as silence and censoring. We need to speak up and speak out to get emotions off our chests; we just need to decide what is best left in our journals and what is worth talking about with your partner.

## LEARN THE LESSONS AND MOVE ON

Using your journal to examine your relationships over your lifetime helps you see and learn lessons about romantic relationships. Start off by writing about what you learned from your first influencers: your parents, siblings, grandparents and extended family; from teachers, friends, youth leaders, neighbours. What did you learn about these relationships from your first job and your colleagues? From your first love, divorce, children, etc.? Do you see any patterns that have come up that you keep repeating? Are there any lessons you once learned that you now know to be no longer true? Is there any baggage it's time to let go of *now*? Is there anything you can be grateful for that has made your current relationship better?

## RESOLVE PROBLEMS EARLY

Don't let molehills become mountains. Deal with them. On a piece of paper or in your journal, draw a line down the centre of the page. On the left-hand side, spend time thinking about areas of the relationship you want to change (depth of connection, time spent together/apart, how you want your needs met, what you aren't talking about that needs to be talked about). Then, on the right-hand side, start writing about what you intend to do about it, how and when you will discuss this. You can also use your journal to plan out surprises, date nights, to remind yourself of things you want to discuss, note down songs or quotes that you want to share, record goals for your relationship, capture what is important to your partner so you can take action (or discuss at a later date), or remind you what really matters. The specific aim is to keep improving your relationship – because in a major longitudinal Harvard study, it was the quality of relationships that contributed most to happiness. For that reason alone, it's worth any effort required.

# Improve romantic relationships

**1** What regular arguments do you have?

**2** How can these be resolved to move forward?

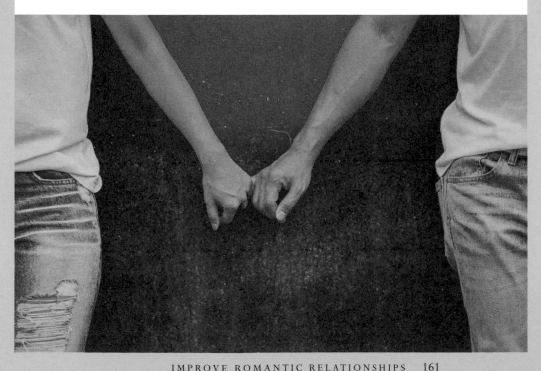

**3** What patterns do you see yourself repeating from your parents' relationship?

**4** What vows or promises did you once make to each other that could worth revisiting?

**5** Where might you be unreasonable or thoughtless in this relationship?

**6** What elephant in the room are you both not currently talking about?

**7** What does romantic love look like to you? And to your partner?

**8** Is there baggage from previous relationships that you could let go of?

**9** What do you want more of in your relationship?

**10** Have you ever tried to make your partner into someone else?

**11** What really matters to your partner? What dreams or ambitions do they have?

**12** Do they feel supported and valued?

**13** What are you grateful for in this relationship?

# 21 Build mental and physical health

'Without health
life is not life,
life is lifeless.'

*Anon*

## Journalling matters to your physical and mental health

I've always been fascinated by what makes people tick – not just mentally but physically – and over the past number of years what neuroscience is discovering makes perfect sense to me. We are only at the beginning of understanding the links between our brains and our bodies, but what we know now is enough to change radically how we act and think. The more I read, the more excited I get – and it's one of the reasons I love journalling so much, because it helps make the links we wouldn't otherwise make. Not only does journalling allow you to be your own alchemist, teacher and coach, there is now overwhelming evidence that it improves your health. This is primarily emotional health, but it will improve your physical health too.

## Take responsibility for your own health

In a world of great healthcare and experts, it's all too easy to abdicate responsibility to others for our health. In the past, when healthcare was so expensive, people took greater care of themselves because going to a doctor was a last resort. Now, in countries where healthcare is free or covered by insurance, we have fallen into the habit of not looking after ourselves as well as we could.

It's time for us to take steps to deliberately improve our own health by journalling. Sports psychologists and coaches know that evidence shows this works to improve performance, as it's a tool to analyze what is working and what isn't, and to measure progress here just as it does elsewhere.

## START NOTICING WHAT IS HAPPENING

Those who specialize in weight loss and fitness also know now that food diaries help people to lose weight. It helps the trainer see unhelpful patterns or to ask questions around the bigger story of days of unhealthy eating or bingeing. The person doing the writing can start to note down what happened and think about the events or emotions that may have triggered this. Evidence shows that getting someone to write about what they eat and their relationship with food can give the insight that leads to change.

## JOURNALLING AND CHRONIC ILLNESS

Those who suffer from a chronic painful condition, or a condition that varies from day to day, have found that keeping journals means they can easily share information with their doctors that helps them to explain how they are really feeling, rate their level of pain, detail their systems or even start to notice any triggers. How often have you gone to your doctor who wants precise details and ended up being vague about how it actually affects you? Well, here's a tool that will help your GP work with you better. Joshua M. Smyth, Associate Professor of Psychology at North Dakota State University, ran a study in 1999 where 47 per cent of patients with asthma and rheumatoid arthritis had symptoms that improved when they wrote about the most traumatic event in their life, even if writing about it was painful to start with. The control group showed a 24 per cent improvement just by writing about their everyday life. Schwartz and Drotar showed it also benefitted people whose child had a chronic illness, so it even helps those whose own health is not directly impacted, but who have to deal with concerns about others.[15]

## IMPROVE YOUR PHYSICAL HEALTH

Even when you journal without these aims in mind, other studies have shown that:

- Journalling can reduce blood pressure.
- Liver function increases.
- Those who journal report having significantly less distress (suffering, sorrow, pain), feel less depressed and have better overall mood.
- Those who journal show fewer symptoms of depression.

- Journalling helps to stop people being overwhelmed by feelings and from feelings being repressed.
- Lung function improves.
- Blood pressure improves.
- Journalling leads to fewer visits to hospital.
- Once admitted to hospital, the number of days spent there is reduced.
- Journalling can lead to an overall increase in wellbeing.
- It can help with recovery from addictions and those who live with alcoholic parents.
- Writing about trauma helps the immune system work better as long as emotions were included.

## PTSD

Journalling reduces flashbacks, nightmares and unexpected memories connected to Post-traumatic Stress Disorder and helps individuals reconnect with activities and/or places they otherwise try to avoid.[16–17] The social psychologist James Pennebaker's early work showed that there was merit in getting someone to write about the same traumatic issue for three or four days for fifteen to twenty minutes at a time. Often this is what gives the breakthrough as the experience is relived from different angles, which either allow the emotions to be processed or allow the individual to distance themselves from the event. Other studies show this technique reduces depression.[18]

## YOUR BEST POSSIBLE SELF

Interesting new research is beginning to show that as well as exploring the past, if you are really interested in improving your mental and physical health, then you should journal about the future. Burton and King suggest that focusing on 'your best possible self' and about the events and experiences that have made you really happy in your life results in very similar health benefits.[19] Research has found that both writing about negative events from different angles and focusing on positive events improved health, happiness and wellbeing. That is significant. Since it's easier and less painful to focus on our positive stories, why not try that as a route to being happier rather than always niggling at an issue from the past? It allows us to move forward more easily while still allowing us to focus on our emotions, boundaries, desires and needs. When we do that, happiness and health follow.

Therefore it makes sense that focusing on the positive is also our greatest weapon against stress and depression, because it changes our thinking. The philosopher and psychologist William James, who died in 1910, was already aware of this when he said, 'The greatest weapon against stress is our ability to choose one thought over another.'

The UK government agency, Health and Safety Executive, defines work-related stress as 'The adverse reaction people have to excessive pressures or other types of demand placed on them at work.' They go on to say that, 'Stress is not an illness – it is a state. However, if stress becomes too excessive and prolonged, mental and physical illness may develop.' The World Health Organization estimates 300 million people worldwide suffer from depression alone. Stress is increasing as a major issue in workplace absence and it is known as a silent killer because it triggers changes in the brain that increase and sustain levels of cortisol; moreover, it usually increases blood pressure.

At some point in our lives, anyone can feel stressed. I suffered extreme work stress in 2006, with symptoms that involved shaking and ringing in my ears, along with the associated sleep deprivation and mental confusion. I've also been stressed by finances and relationships in the past. For you, it might be the thought of Christmas or other holidays looming, and that to-do list that keeps growing, or it could be a major birthday or a loved one's illness or any other life event. Whatever the trigger, you will know the thoughts and feelings that come with it.

I've used journals for many years, but in 2006 I returned to journalling and found again how powerful it can be. Though counselling reminded me how my thinking was affecting me, it was the work I did in my journals that helped me change things. I realized nearly all of the stress I was experiencing was down to my own emotional state. I was focusing on what wasn't working instead of what *was* working. I was imagining the worst-case scenarios. I felt helpless, overwhelmed, useless and upset at my feelings of a lack of control or power. I realized I was not living in the present but focused either on the future or the past. My journal helped by providing me with a way of looking objectively and clearly at the thoughts that were swirling around in my head. I was later to find that scientific evidence overwhelmingly supports its use:

- Klein and Boals report it helps your working memory (often reduced when stressed) and it's also effective for post-traumatic stress disorder (which was also backed up by studies after the Hurricane Katrina disaster in 2005).[16]
- Park and Blumberg say that it increases emotional wellbeing.[20]
- Smyth, Hockemeyer and Tulloch report that those who journal suffer significantly less pain and suffering and experience a better mood overall.[21]

And the good thing is that it doesn't matter what age, race or sex you are for you to feel the benefits of journalling – although it could benefit men slightly more as they find it harder to talk about their emotions.

## USING A STRESS JOURNAL

The psychologist James Pennebaker says that '… disclosure helps us find meaning in complicated life circumstances … writing helps to reconstruct painful thoughts and images into a story or narrative. Once we can give an upsetting event some degree of structure with a clear beginning, middle and an end we are better able to move past it.' Ultimately, while medication sometimes helps, more often than not it just dulls the pain, because unless you take action to deal with the situation that is causing you stress, it will not go away. You may find avoidance techniques, but it's so much better to take action, even if that means ultimately leaving a job or a house or a relationship, or if you can't do that, finding ways to change how you think about it is critical.

Keeping a stress journal works in a number of ways:

- Helps you identify why you are stressed.
- Breaks big chunks into little ones to see progress and help keep you calm.
- If you tend to concentrate on painful episodes rather than positive ones, or if you make mountains out of molehills, it can show you're not seeing the big picture. Sometimes perspective is all it takes.
- Reveals triggers of certain moods or reactions so you can avoid them in the future – or find better ways to deal with them.
- Allows you to see that when you felt particularly negative, you still survived.
- Helps you avoid unnecessary stress (the things you feel you must do but when you look at them, you often don't) and it helps you be more assertive to say no to things that are not your responsibility.
- Reframe problems in a different way.
- Manages your time better *and* builds in time for relaxation.
- Helps you learn to say no to things you don't want to do, or when you feel overwhelmed.
- Shows you the unhealthy ways you are possibly dealing with your stress.
- Illuminates your perfectionist tendencies, and helps you be gentler on yourself, and even learn compromise; this is a major cause of stress and it's all under your control.
- By noting down feelings and symptoms, you can also use it to help you discuss how you feel with your GP, occupational health worker, your line manager or HR.

Neuroscientist Richard Davidson says you find ways to be healthier and happier when you learn to think differently, when you start to take control again. So writing a stress journal is not enough. You need to have a balance so that not everything you write about is stressful. A 'stress' journal also needs to be a gratitude journal, where you end the day focusing on the good things that happened that day. There are always, always, things to be grateful for.

# Build mental and physical health

1 What steps could you take to improve your health?

2 What currently isn't working well for you?

3 What patterns or triggers do you have that sabotage your desire to live in a healthy way?

4 Which type of professional could support you in writing about trauma?

5 What would your 'best possible self' look like?

6 In which circumstances do you feel helpless?

7 Where do you feel stuck? What could get you unstuck?

8 Where and when do you feel stressed?

9 What happens when you feel stressed?

10 What unhealthy ways do you deal with stress?

11 How much of what you do is unnecessary or could be done by someone else if you asked for help?

**12** Do you need to be more assertive so you can say no to things that are not your responsibility?

**13** How could you reframe your current problem?

**14** How can you be gentler on yourself, or learn to compromise?

**15** What's good in your life?

## And, on a sheet of paper or in a blank journal:

Make a list of actions you could take to live a healthier life (by what you do or no longer do). Pick one to start doing.

## Choose a positive mood word for a daily affirmation:

Some examples could be: 'healthy', 'calm', 'peace', 'love', 'learning', 'balance', 'recovery', 'healing', 'wellbeing', 'strength'.

# 22 Be authentic

'I wish I could show you when you are lonely or in darkness, the astonishing light of your own being.'

*Hafiz*

### Let your light shine

I filed these words away in my head and spent months thinking about the power, freedom and hope that they represented, particularly in the dark times when it is hard to see what we bring to the world. While I had certainly experienced darkness – both the dark side of who I was and the dark side of life – to think of my being as being 'astonishing' and 'light' was at once uplifting and frightening, because it was hard to believe. In a world of 'Be quiet' and 'Don't do', and 'What will people say?' and 'Don't show off', we aren't encouraged to shine; but the Persian poet Hafiz's words challenge us to forget all that and serve the world best by just being who we are.

Too often, we allow our ego or false pride to reject what we've been given or who we are, or we live our lives on other people's terms because they have told us that is how we should live. So even if we are actually filled with the 'astonishing light of our own being', we hide it – and when we do this, the world loses out. When I thought about this, with my journal, exploring whether it was true for everyone (and it was just me that was excluded), or if it was true for only the elite, the people who had made it, who had never failed, I knew Hafiz meant everyone – no exclusions. And if this was true for me, what did it mean for how I lived personally?

Acclaimed lecturer, activist and bestselling author Marianne Williamson writes in her book, *Return To Love*, about how we stop ourselves shining so others won't feel insecure – and says there is nothing enlightened about living in that way. It stops us from living from a place of wholeness and power and contribution and it does the same for others, because they too are afraid to let us see who they really are. Slowly, my attitude started to change about how I lived.

## TAKING THE MASKS OFF

I started to think about how someone would live who thought of themselves in this way. What difference would it make to what they did or said? What if this was the truth about who they were, not what others expected them to be? If I believed this about myself, then surely it must change how I was supposed to be living. I could be aligned with what I really valued in life instead of wearing masks all the time, the same masks I had become accustomed to wearing and that were slowly suffocating me in the process. If I was going to be real then it meant no more clown faces with painted-on smiles (to hide the fact I was unhappy or angry underneath) and no more perfect porcelain dolls. It meant no more superhero outfits and no more masks – but I'd forgotten that without the mask and the outfit, the superhero is always an ordinary person. Yet Hafiz is saying exactly that: you are an ordinary person, in the middle of an ordinary life – but you are also extraordinary with that lightness inside. It is in our very ordinariness that we became real.

What a way to live life! By the time I was thirty-five, I was beginning to crack under the weight of the masks I was wearing. As is the way with midlife crises, at the same time came a realization that if we are granted a lifespan of seventy, then I was halfway to the end of my life without ever really being free to be me. I found myself asking lots of questions. I'd subsumed myself for so long I had ended up standing on a pedestal of my own making. Who was I under all the masks I had chosen to wear? Why did I feel the need to be perfect? Why did I not say what I really felt or wanted? It was a wonderfully shocking realization a few years later to find that I wasn't any of the masks I wore. And yet I had been allowing the masks to define me, believing they made me more powerful when in fact they kept me living someone else's life by pretending.

## KNOW YOURSELF, BE YOURSELF

Ancient Chinese philosopher and writer Lao Tzu said, 'Intelligent people know others – enlightened people know themselves.' Your journal allows you to know yourself and it holds you accountable, when you write honestly. You might start off by writing about how wonderful a day it was and how great you are feeling, but it will soon remind you again to be real, sometimes even by the words that 'mistakenly' show up on the page that you didn't expect yourself to write. Journalling allows you to observe yourself, write out your emotions and your darkest thoughts, as well as reflecting on your day, deciding what you could have done differently, what you need to change, or what you did really well. You will start to recognize the parts of you that have developed because you have unconsciously copied patterns of behaviour you have seen or been part of, or what is accepted as the 'norm' in your family or community and is simply learned behaviour you can unlearn.

As a child, I learned to be quiet, to avoid conflict, and I carried this into other significant relationships where I avoided conflict, didn't stand up for myself, acted as peacemaker when I shouldn't have and even apologized for things I hadn't done if I felt it cleared the atmosphere. I put on masks to negate my own emotions. It is little wonder then that I chose relationships that mirrored that part of me. Therefore, for me, living authentically means I acknowledge how I am feeling, deal with the root issue and then find healthy ways to express anger, hurt or sorrow, so I experience these emotions while doing the least harm possible to others.

## USING YOUR JOURNAL
Ask yourself the reasons why you don't shine your light and write them down. Because every time you hide your true self from others, when you settle for less than amazing, less than fantastic – you deny the fact that you are fantastic! You hide your light when you dumb down your intelligence and dismiss your abilities. Ask yourself what masks you wear and if you are willing instead to live with integrity and honour yourself, to live, act and think in ways that are true to your spiritual self and to let your true self shine.

What is stopping you living the life you want now? Why are you afraid of showing your emotion? Why you are settling for less? If you think you are settling for less, what does aiming for more look like to you? Are you willing to define or redefine who you are rather than have others box you in? How would your life be different if you were always true to yourself, to your values? What would it mean to you if you were to connect with people at a level where you share your true self and hide nothing, where you take those risks?

## FLY FREE
Are you willing to be free and be happier? In order to take risks, are you willing to make mistakes and learn from them, and put in the daily effort that living authentically can sometimes mean until it really becomes your norm? Are you willing to do this at work *and* at home, so you are always who you are wherever you are,

because authenticity isn't something you put on and off like a coat, although you can decide what information to share in each setting? Are you willing to be responsible for your life, knowing your limitations while also knowing your gifts and abilities and using them? To take all your masks off and be yourself, dark side, light side, warts and all? If you do this, you will find that you are serving the world and you're no longer exhausted trying to be someone you never were. It is worth the effort because of the joy and freedom it brings. There is no better time than now to understand who you really are, accept that or change what you want to change – and then shine. It is no longer about trying to be somebody; you don't need to be anybody else but you – and there is no effort required in being yourself.

# Be authentic

1 Who are you, right now, without your masks?

2 What are you *not* contributing to the world by hiding who you really are?

3 Have you managed to keep pleasing all the people around you so far, all of the time? If so, why continue?

4 Are you honest with others?

5 What do you think others think of you?

6  What is it that you are afraid to let others see?

7  Are you fully you wherever you are and whatever you are doing?

8  What are your core values and how do you express these on a daily basis?

9  What really matters to you?

10  What do you want to stop doing?

11  Where might you dare to be different?

**12** Do you need to consider interim steps for this?

**13** Do you take responsibility for your life?

**14** What do you want most from life?

**15** What do you want to start doing?

**16** If not now, when?

## Choose a thought to concentrate on from the choices below:

'Be yourself; everyone else is already taken.' *Oscar Wilde*

'Own who you are.' *Anon*

'The privilege of a lifetime is to become who you truly are.'

*Carl Jung*

**Be remarkable**

**Thinking differently**

Some years ago, a training team came into my work and challenged us to think differently. There were a number of 'dare to' cards and we were asked to choose a few that resonated with us and then consider what they meant to us in more depth. You could try this in your journal and think about what these might mean to you:

- Dare to have fun.
- Dare to be present.
- Dare to be different.
- Dare to be authentic.
- Dare to be remarkable.

The dares generated a lot of discussion about how hard they would be to try or sustain. What fascinated me was that nearly everyone agreed not only was 'Dare to be remarkable' the hardest, it was the one most people weren't even prepared to try. It boiled down to the fact that it seemed a step too far. In a corporate environment, where people often feel boxed in by particular requirements, many felt that they could cope with being different – but none wanted to be remarkable. Reasons given included, 'It would be too hard to keep up', 'It would make you stand out' and 'It would mean I could never make a mistake'. It seemed that it was much easier to be like 'most people' than it was to be remarkable. Even those who were happy to be different (and stand out for their desire not to be seen as one of the crowd) couldn't see themselves being remarkable; it was too high a price to pay.

## START AT THE VERY BEGINNING

If you've ever considered this option and said you can't dare to be remarkable, that is nothing more than a big lie that your ego tells you. Wanting to be like 'most people' means you are settling for less than you can be. It means you are hiding your uniqueness and what makes you wonderfully you. You are choosing to limit your life, and that means you are not living the life you really want to live, and you won't ever have quite the impact on the world you long to have or could have. Is it worth the risk to try it? Stay with me and consider it. If you decide to dare to be remarkable but don't quite know where to start, then start at the very beginning. As *The Sound of Music*'s Maria would say, 'It's a very good place to start!' Start where you are now and make a difference by what you say and do straight away – it's remarkable in itself how many people keep waiting to do things until conditions are 'right' as an excuse to keep themselves where they are. Those people in society who are remarkable are the ones who are open to what life offers to them, who respond to needs and seek to resolve them, who take risks and make plans and persist in achieving them. And this represents more than any definition of success.

## THE DIFFERENCE THAT MAKES THE DIFFERENCE

Since 2004, *The Times* newspaper in the UK has drawn up a list of people the general public consider to be remarkable for the way their power, talent or moral example is transforming the world. It's worth a read as you don't often get the opportunity to hear about these people, all of whom are doing amazing things. Yet the thing is I'm quite sure that hardly *any* of them believe they are particularly 'remarkable' and that for me is the critical thing – they are all following their passions. They are just doing what they know they need to do because 'somebody needed to do something'. They are doing what they love to do anyway, doing the next obvious thing they need to do because there is a gap in the market or a need that isn't being fulfilled, or they are just doing their job, but in a remarkable way. They are not concerned about standing out unless this means people notice them for what they are doing and can make a contribution. They aren't defined by any failures or detours along the way, as those have led them to where they ultimately wanted to be. They don't give much time to thinking about not being able to 'keep it up' because what they do isn't generalized out to all parts of their life – they are just focused on being remarkable in the particular area they are noted for.

They do what they do really well (though not perfectly) and serve their clients, end users or other businesses in doing so. They do this by challenging the status quo and doing something different – but it was that difference that made the difference. That is also *my* definition of remarkable.

## A REMARKABLE BIRD

One of the best stories you will ever read is *Jonathan Livingston Seagull*. You may have already realized that Jonathan is an important bird because he is being called by his full name (just like when you were little and when your parents used your full name, you always knew you were in trouble). However, no one thought he was important. They didn't pay him much attention but when they did, they found that he kept challenging the norm and that frightened them enough to avoid him.

He was just a seagull after all and seagulls were supposed to fly in a particular way. Everyone knew that: his parents, his peers and the 'wise ones' who ruled the flock. It had always been that way, for generations and generations, and it made life easier to know the rules and live by them. Jonathan had his life mapped out for him. Yet deep down, he had a problem with this, because when he flew, he knew that what they said wasn't entirely true. So he refused to accept that he had to behave exactly like all the other seagulls. He knew he could be remarkable if he just tried hard enough, pushed the boundaries and pushed himself higher, faster, further – and he went for it. He achieved what he set out to achieve – but was rejected by his flock and isolated by his first tribe. In fact, he was completely ostracized and his parents – not wanting to stand out – went along with all the other seagulls. What a price to pay for being remarkable.

At this point Jonathan had a choice. He could stay small and be like everyone else and have their approval and acceptance – or he could refuse to accept that certain things weren't possible. He looked sadly at all the others, who were not prepared to challenge the norm, who were happy to settle for being less than they could be. He didn't think he was better than them and he wasn't cocky or self-important; he just knew that he was capable of more, just as he believed every one of the other seagulls were too. He knew that there was more to life than he had currently experienced and he wanted to live his life large! So he kept going, he practised, focused, learned from his mistakes – and made the decision not to accept life as it was or as everyone else accepted it. He decided to follow his own path, dance to his own tune and soar in his own way.

## CHOOSE YOUR FUTURE

There are many famous examples of people who chose to be remarkable. They didn't set out to do this, but as they followed their path with determination and challenged the norms, they found themselves in situations where they made remarkable choices. People like Nelson Mandela, Esther Rantzen, Rosa Parks and Erin Brockovich. And there millions of others who have made similar choices and are not at all famous. There are the parents who have suffered the loss of a child and then founded charities or raised thousands of pounds to help others, those who have lobbied for changes in the law (like Sarah's Law or Lillian's Law) or battled life-threatening or limiting disease and yet raised funds for others. It's the unpaid carers who look after members of their families at home, the foster parents, those who organize lunches for the elderly or homeless, those who become involved in their communities, those who create a better future following a past that has involved crime or addiction, or those who create legacies of love. I am privileged to know many remarkable people who do exactly these things.

A fantastic young woman I know came from difficult background with an alcoholic father she rarely saw, who hit her mother regularly. (In fact, she has no memories before she was eight, as she has just shut off that part of her life.) When I met her, her mother was HIV-positive and had attempted suicide twice, and her brother was addicted to heroin. This single mum with two lovely girls, who had spent a lot of time trying to support all of her family, had a vision of opening up a range of safe places for children, somewhere they could go and just be loved and accepted. She knew how it felt not to have that and could have focused her energy on what she hadn't been given in life, but she wanted to have a different future. So every morning she got up and did one hundred skips, repeating positive affirmations to herself because she knew she needed to actively cut off all the negative voices she heard in her head, from her grandfather telling her she'd never achieve anything in her life to her mother agreeing. Back then, she was already remarkable, for her energy, her ability to put her past behind her, in what she had achieved for herself and her children, and because of her greater vision.

## DARE TO BE REMARKABLY YOU

So will you dare to be remarkable? Will you take the challenge to try and fail and learn from your experiences? If you use your journal to help you stay true to yourself, *you* will be the difference that makes the difference. It will allow you to start wondering how you might be uniquely you – and then determine how to honour that. Once you have a definition that satisfies for now then start where you are. You might decide to go with the flow of life, or you might create specific goals and steps, or have a general vision of what you want and then be open to how you actually get there. Think what being remarkable means to you in your working life, social life and relationships, and the fears you have about that definition.

After all, if you were to be remarkable, what would you see in your life? What would you feel, what sounds would you hear? Where would you be living, what people would be around you, what clothes would you be wearing? Jack Canfield visualized himself being an international speaker and even got business cards printed as if he was already doing it – a year before he actually did. Richard Branson always knew he was going to be a tycoon; he says he knew that if you really believed something, you would achieve it.

Take control of your thought processes; I've covered this before, but research shows that a positive attitude is a powerful thing. Be positive. Work on your inner critic as much as you need to, using positive affirmations if you need to – but don't break your neck or your spirit doing so! Being remarkable comes at a cost and part of that cost is for you to remember that it starts with your thoughts and it is *your* responsibility to control them.

Ask the right questions. The right question asked at the right time can make all the difference in the world. It may make a huge difference to an organization, or a person. Don't assume others are asking the right questions; be courageous and ask any question you need to ask. And don't be afraid to ask the hard questions, the ones you need to ask but that you sometimes put off asking because you may be afraid of the answer and what that might mean next. They are also the questions you need to ask those closest to you, when you really care about them; when you don't really have the choice to ignore things. I'm so grateful for those friends that I trust who ask me the hard questions – like 'Why are you doing so much?' or 'Why are you doing what you are doing (or not doing what you should be doing)?' and who ask me questions about my 'wisdom' or actions at a certain time.

## PUSH THOSE BOUNDARIES

Boundaries are not there just to keep people safe; sometimes they exist to keep people locked in, so always be prepared to push boundaries relating to personal effectiveness or achievement, particularly if society imposes them. Amelia Earhart was the first woman to fly solo across the Atlantic – at a time when most women didn't even drive, let alone fly! Sprinter Wilma Rudolph won Olympic medals in the 1950s and 1960s, even though as a child she could hardly walk as a result of her limp. Lech Walesa founded Solidarity in Poland in 1980 – and 3,000 women defied the tanks and passed out Solidarity literature and flowers. Social activist Helen Keller achieved great things despite being profoundly deaf and blind, refusing to let that impact her ability to live life to the full or her work to make the lives of other blind and deaf people better. Talk show host Oprah Winfrey learned to turn deeply negative childhood experiences into a way of helping others – and has made a huge impact on millions. And Falklands hero Simon Weston has refused to see himself as some do ('sadly, badly burned and disfigured'), but declares he is actually incredibly gifted and very, very lucky. Anyone who has ever broken any record, invented anything or changed something knows that there comes a time when you take a risk. That is when you no longer settle for less or just enough, when you dare to be remarkable – that is when the world changes.

# Be remarkable

1 In which circumstances do you settle for being like 'most people'?

2 When do you stop yourself from shining by staying small?

3 Who says you can't be remarkable?

4 What does being remarkable look like to you, in your working life, social life and relationships?

5 Why is it hard for you to consider being remarkable?

**6** What if that belief wasn't true?

**7** What would happen if you did fail?

**8** What boundaries is it time to push?

**9** Where are you seeing limitations?

**10** What frustrates you that you know you could do better?

**11** Where are you existing or surviving, rather than living?

**12** What rules are you accepting or living by without challenging?

**13** Who owns the rules you live by?

**14** If not now, when?

## And, in a blank journal:

Reflect on what you've learned by stepping up. What were the results? What worked? What didn't work? What could you do differently next time? What are you not able to do yet?

## Choose a thought to concentrate on from the choices below:

'There is only one way to avoid criticism: Do nothing, say nothing, and be nothing.' *Aristotle*

It's OK to stand out for excellence. I can dare to be remarkable.

'If the only prayer you said in your whole life was, "thank you", that would suffice.'

*Meister Eckhart*

# 24 Be grateful

**The one thing you can do to change your life**

I don't know who came up with the 'attitude of gratitude' concept. It has been attributed to many people, including the Dalai Lama, and will make a difference in your life — or it could change it completely. 'Yeah, but,' I hear you say. You can't be grateful because your life is either pretty lousy or you are doing just fine as you are, or you're holding it together right now because so much in your life is going wrong. Your life is too busy, you're too stressed, your relationships are falling apart, you're too anxious about yesterday and worried about tomorrow to think about this in your journal and, actually, you're prepared to settle for less right now because the only thing you can be grateful for is sleep. It's not realistic to be grateful.

I don't care if it's not realistic, it's the one thing that will improve the quality of your life more than anything else. In fact, it is critical to develop this habit and practice if you want your life to improve. You need to start writing a gratitude journal. It's the best way I know of that enables you to take control of your own happiness. Your emotions are your responsibility; you are not bound by them or held in sway to them OR what is going on in your life.

Developing an attitude of gratitude will improve your physical and mental health, help you change how you think, help you practice finding silver linings or gifts in less than totally positive events. When you look for reasons to be cheerful then you won't be obsessing about yourself and the situation. You will be looking outside of yourself and that is where you can see options and possibilities.

## OPTIMISM VERSUS PESSIMISM

The vast majority of children are full of energy, curiosity and positivity. Your genetic predisposition may be to be an optimist or a pessimist, but the good news is that it isn't fixed on this particular scale; you can increase your 'set point' by up to 50 per cent depending on your thoughts and habits. Regardless of where you start, why not choose to be happier or more optimistic – it's a learned skill. We can do so many things to change how we feel and that starts with our thoughts. Too often, negativity is a habit that develops over time. Two people can experience exactly the same event and yet one will view it negatively and one more positively. This is about more than just your nature, it's a choice, and as Viktor E. Frankl said, the ability to choose our attitude is 'the last of the human freedoms'.

In my courses, I sometimes run a version of an exercise devised by Bartlett and McCullough to show the power of gratitude. For the first two weeks, I ask attendees to record their difficulties and how they feel. Then I ask them to record what they are grateful for and note how they feel. Every single delegate feels worse when they focus on what isn't working and better for recording their gratitude. When the researchers concluded their study in 2003, they noted that those who focused on gratitude were more optimistic, exercised more and reported fewer health issues, felt stronger themselves *and* offered others a greater degree of emotional support.

## JUST LOOK AT YOUR OWN LIFE

You don't have time to be envious or resentful of someone else's happiness because if you're focusing on that then you aren't spending time ensuring your own happiness. Gratitude is a key way of changing how you feel and you only have to do it 'once a week or three times a week for six weeks', according to a 2005 study reported in the *Review of General Psychology*, for it to have an impact. Being grateful for 'what is', for what we have, instead of comparing ourselves to others and looking for the differences, is better for our health – and our lives. So if you've wondered whether you could change the world, start with gratitude. If you want to change *your* world, and be happier, start with gratitude too! It changed my life. As writer and former pharmaceutical scientist Dr David Hamilton says:

'Gratitude research is showing that gratitude brings us a more loving feeling, as well as more joy, enthusiasm, happiness, optimism and even better physical health. Robert Emmons [the world's leading scientific expert on gratitude] points out that gratitude also reduces destructive impulses like greed, envy, resentment, bitterness and hostility and helps us to cope better with the stresses and strains of everyday life. Show me a drug that can do all this in a one-tablet-a-day form!'

# Be grateful

1 What are you grateful for?

2 What do other people do that you are grateful for? How can you pass
that on to others?

**3** Even where you are facing challenges, what can you still be grateful for?

## Answer these questions based on those by Robert Emmons:

**1** What do you typically take for granted?

**2** What would your life be like without this person/event/circumstance that you take for granted?

**3** How would you feel if you were to be deprived of a small routine pleasure?

**4** Think about something you desired for a long time, that you then received but were not grateful for. Why was that?

**5** Identify non-grateful thoughts: for example, thinking you deserve better; that life is boring and monotonous; that things have not turned out the way you wanted. Are these helping or hindering your sense of happiness?

## And:

Write a gratitude letter to someone from your past. You don't need to post or deliver it (or you may be unable to do so), but you can if you want to.

Write a gratitude letter to someone in your present-day life and give it to them – better still, arrange to meet for a coffee and read it to them.

Say thank you to people who don't always get thanked – those who deliver public services, or who serve you in a shop or restaurant.

## Choose a thought to concentrate on from the choices below:

I am grateful for so much in my life. Thank you, thank you, thank you.

I am grateful for all my teachers.

# 25 *Dare to be happier*

'The greater part of our happiness or misery depends upon our dispositions, and not upon our circumstances.'

*Martha Washington*

### Your life has nothing to do with luck

While there are many reasons to journal, the ultimate reason lies in the one thing we all want – to be happier. Robert Wiseman, author of *The Luck Factor*, concluded that the one thing that will make a difference in your life – for success luck, and life in general – is not luck, it is having a positive attitude. He says we make our own luck and that it is a myth that people are happy and successful because life was handed to them on a plate.

It is as much a myth as thinking that those who are happy and successful have never had any problems to deal with. Let's face it, how much do you really know about others? How do you know they haven't had to deal with significant issues in their lives? How do you know that they haven't been bullied, been in an unhappy marriage, are living with a broken heart, have mental health or addiction issues, either themselves or in their family, lost loved ones, survived abuse, are living with significant debt problems or are about to face financial ruin? Even when you think you know people, you will only ever get part of their story.

I can guarantee that some of the happiest people you know will be living with exactly the same problems you are living with now or will have dealt with them in the past.

## LIVING IN THE REAL WORLD

So aren't you just a little curious how people like this can still live in the real world and yet remain happy and content? Was it because of what they read or did, thought or said to themselves, or was it their friends, their background, their character or embracing a particular faith? Or could it be that they broke free of their fears or learned to push through them? Did they take little incremental steps to change, stretching comfort zones and beliefs – or did they choose to radically change their attitude?

## THE DIFFERENCE THAT MAKES THE DIFFERENCE

Your happiness comes down to what you think, feel and do. In *The How of Happiness: A Scientific Approach to Getting the Life You Want*, Sonja Lyubomirsky's research shows happiness is about 50 per cent determined by genetics. This is the happiness set point. Just 10 per cent comes from the things we think will make us happy (and where we spend our energy) – things like wealth, living conditions, relationships, occupation and possessions. That's actually a tiny proportion when you consider the other 40 per cent comes from our habits, behaviours, the decisions we make and how we think.

Therefore our happiness is much more down to us than we'd like to believe. It happens when we take control of our attitude and thoughts, which affect our feelings, and when we make a decision to choose a positive outlook, or to do what it takes to be happier. Too often, our lives reflect our unwillingness to consciously choose the life we create. We choose to remain unhappy because we don't challenge our thoughts or think about what we are doing or why, we don't set boundaries, we aren't honest with people and we do what others expect us to do. Everyone wants to be happier – but we don't dare to do what it takes.

## KNOW WHAT MAKES YOU HAPPY!

I know what makes me happy and it isn't the 'big' things: the seaside, kittens, ducklings, sunshine, snowball fights, being cosy, log fires, my electric blanket, rain, walking in the forest or hills or beside the sea, a great book, good wine, spending time with friends who support and uplift me, making dinner and seeing everyone enjoy eating it, live music and concerts, picnics, *Anne of Green Gables*, *It's a Wonderful Life*, *Seabiscuit*, *Top Gun*, *The Last Samurai*, *A Knight's Tale*, facials, massages, candles, classical music, saxophones, watching and listening to waves crashing on the shore, go-karting, paintball, walking the dog, *Extreme Makeover: Home Edition*, Gordon Ramsay and Jamie Oliver, good food, cooking, canoeing, the hot tub, travelling to new places, fruit-and-nut chocolate, swimming, ice-cream sundaes, real pizza, window shopping, shoes, handbags, writing, helping others, giving, apple pie, Eve's pudding, when I express my creativity, a clean organized house, phone calls, letters and cards from friends … and that's just for starters!

What makes *me* happy won't be what makes *you* happy. When I ask people on my Dare to be Happier courses to list what makes them happy, many really struggle to write down five things, let alone thirty. If you've never taken the time before to think about what makes you happy, do it now, because life is too short to be (or stay) unhappy – and it's too short to keep your Sunday clothes for 'best'. You might find you need to go back in your life to find out what used to make you happy and resurrect some things that have been lost because your life has become too busy. If life is what happens while we are busy making other plans, then maybe we better plan some happiness into today: make your happiness your priority.

Learn not just to find your own happiness but to make your own happiness whenever and however. Stop waiting for other people to make you happy. When you depend on other people to make you happy, or expect them to, you risk being disappointed. When you expect others to do this, you also place a huge burden on their shoulders and this is unfair as no one can truly make you happier. Happiness is an internal process that involves your mind and heart, even when people act in ways that could make you deeply unhappy (and if you have significant people in your life who do that, then start making choices about how you stand up for yourself because you deserve to be treated with love and respect). Don't continue to let them control your happiness by their words and actions.

## HAPPINESS AND OTHER EMOTIONS

You have choices about how strong, less than totally positive emotions affect you. I'm not saying that we decide to suppress these, quite the contrary, as it is vital for our happiness to process all our emotions. Nor am I saying that we should ignore them because to do that is to say we are not human. But sometimes we get stuck in a particular emotion because we fear what is ahead, or we don't want to feel any more pain than we already are, instead of allowing ourselves to go through the emotions and get to the other side. And we must stop believing that there is only one way to express our emotions or that it isn't acceptable to do so. Take grief, for example. In some cultures, when someone dies, there are no tears at all because friends and family focus on the new life that person now has. In other cultures, there are set times in the calendar to grieve (one week, one month and one year after the death). In

Ireland, there are week-long or three-day wakes where people share a combination of tears and laughter as a life is celebrated and remembered. It is not so long ago that the Victorians had huge, theatrical funerals where everyone dressed solely in black and the mourning went on for a year afterwards.

These different approaches demonstrate that our reaction to life-changing events like the death of a loved one can be different purely because of the culture we are brought up in. If that is the case, then how we think, and even how we are expected to think and react, is to an extent a choice we make (whether consciously or unconsciously). I read of a woman who chose not to be overwhelmed by grief because it wasn't what her husband would have wanted. She said that choosing to be happy – or to accept happiness where she was able to find it – was a better option than choosing to be miserable. She forced herself to go to parties and social events, even when she didn't want to leave the house, and then found that well-meaning friends and family couldn't accept what she was doing. They expected her to be 'in mourning' publicly for much longer than she appeared to be and told her what she was doing wasn't right, even though it was for her – and it was what her husband would have wanted.

## HOW TO HANDLE NEGATIVE EMOTIONS

*All* emotions are a part of life and can't be avoided, although we often try to do that, particularly with intense emotions; we avoid them directly, pretend they don't exist or we numb them. If we think too negatively about particular events, people or thoughts, it makes us anxious, worried or depressed.

As human beings, we need emotions to keep us safe, to be fully human, and to process life events (like grieving helps us process loss). So sometimes you need to recognize and name the emotion you are feeling, then just allow it to happen, finding a way to vent it in a healthy way – and remember that no emotion lasts for ever. Some ways to handle these are to:

- Accept the emotion and go with the flow. Accept that you are meant to be feeling it for now.
- Remind yourself that all emotions pass; this is an important step.
- Remind yourself that just because you feel this emotion it doesn't make it the truth or your reality.
- Distract yourself and stay busy.
- Check out the language you are using, as words can change your emotional state, and choose words with less intensity.
- Reframe your thinking.

- Exercise.
- Sleep.
- Choose not to avoid or numb the feeling by avoidance, withdrawing, suppressing or getting stuck.
- Talk to supportive people (remembering that to do this excessively will keep you stuck in the story and the emotion).
- Ask yourself, 'What could I do right now that would help me feel better?'
- Start trusting yourself to have confidence in your ability to cope with challenges – you've got this far, remember!
- Be gentle on yourself and show self-compassion.
- Ask for support and build a supportive tribe.
- Believe you can face your fears and even though you are feeling frightened, you can learn from anything.

## CHOOSE YOUR STATE

If we create our own reality, then why not create a happier, abundant life? Our state of mind affects our physiology too, because when we speak or think in certain ways, chemical messengers are released that travel through our bodies. When our thoughts are negative, angry or upset, our immune system is depressed. The opposite is also true – so in choosing happier thoughts, we also choose to be healthier.

## BE KIND TO OTHERS, BE KIND TO YOURSELF

As well as choosing your thoughts (which includes living in the present) and developing your attitude of gratitude, the other part of the triad of happiness habits is being kind to yourself and others. You will find that you are increasingly happy as you actually 'do good', blessing others with your time, your money, your energy or even your knowledge. Being kind to yourself means giving up perfection for excellence, eliminating negative things and people from your life, finding affirmations that work for you, learning to love yourself and doing what you love. Life starts now, there are no dress rehearsals: dare to be happier.

# Dare to be happier

1 What used to make you happy?

2 When were you happiest?

3 What makes you happy now?

4 What one thing would you change that would mean you would be happier?

5 Do you keep postponing your happiness to a more suitable time?

**6** What habits are stopping you from being happier?

**7** What could you learn to accept that would help you be happier?

**8** What excuses are you using for not taking the steps you know you need to take to be happier?

## And, on a sheet of paper or in a blank journal:

Make a list of one hundred things that make you happy, or could make you happier, and commit to ticking them off.

Choose four habits that would make you happier. American Founding Father Benjamin Franklin picked thirteen 'virtues' that he wanted more of in his life and then concentrated on one each week. He knew that when he defined his target, he hugely increased his chances of hitting it.

Do a Happiness SWOT (Strengths, Weaknesses, Opportunities, Threats) Analysis. Organizations use SWOT analysis to determine their strategy for the next three or five years, so do that for your own happiness. Look at areas in your life that are already strong as well as those where you are weaker and work out changes you could make. Consider external issues that might affect your plans to be happier and make an action plan to deal with those. Now start looking for opportunities to dare to be happier!

# Index

(Page numbers in **bold** refer to main concepts)

# Bibliography

[1] Greenberg, M. A., Wortman, C. B. & Stone, A. A. (1996) Emotional expression and physical heath. *Journal of Personality and Social Psychology*, 71, 588–602.

[2] Smyth, J. M. (1998) Written emotional expression. *Journal of Consulting and Clinical Psychology*, 66, 174–184.

[3] Spera, S. P., Buhrfeind, E. D. & Pennebaker, J. W. (1994) Expressive writing and coping with job loss. *Academy of Management Journal*, 37, 722–733.

[4] Pennebaker, J. W. & Francis, M. E. (1996) Cognitive, emotional, and language processes in disclosure. *Cognition and Emotion*, 10, 601–626.

[5] McCrindle, A. R. & Christensen, C. A. (1995) The impact of learning journals. *Learning and Instruction*, 5(2), 167–185.

[6] Boud, D., Keogh, R. & Walker, D. (Eds) (1985) Reflection. *London: Kogan Page*.

[7] Mezirow, J. (1997) Transformative Learning. *New Directions for Adult & Continuing Education*, 74, 5–12.

[8] Scott, V. B., Robare, R. D., Raines, D. B. *et al* (2003) Emotive writing moderates the relationship. *North American Journal of Psychology*, 5, 311–324.

[9] O'Connor, M., Nikoletti, S., Kristjanson, L. J. *et al* (2003) Writing therapy for the bereaved. *Journal of Palliative Medicine*, 6, 195–204.

[10] Lattanzi, M. & Hale, M.E. (1985) Giving Grief Words. *OMEGA: Journal of Death and Dying*, 15(1), 45–52.

[11] Flett, G.L., Nepon, T. & Hewitt, P.L. (2015) Perfectionism, Worry, and Rumination. *Perfectionism, Health and Well-being*, 121–155.

[12] Odou, N. & Brinker, J. (2014) Exploring the relationship between rumination, self-compassion, and mood. *Self and Identity*, 13(4), 449–459.

[13] Lepore, S. J. & Greenberg, M. A. (2002) Mending broken hearts. *Psychology and Health*, 17, 547–560.

[14] Slatcher, R.B. & Pennebaker, J.W. (2006) How do I love thee? *Psychological Science* 17(8), 660–4.

[15] Schwartz, L. & Drotar, D. (2004) Effects of written emotional disclosure. *Journal of Pediatric Psychology*, 29, 105–118.

[16] Klein, K. & Boals, A. (2001) Expressive writing can increase working memory capacity. *Journal of Experimental Psychology: General*, 130, 520–533.

[17] Sloan, D. M. & Marx, B. P. (2004b) Taking pen to hand. *Clinical Psychology: Science and Practice*, 11, 121–137.

[18] Krpan, K.M., Kross, E., Berman, M.G., Deldin, P.J., Askren, M.K. & Jonides, J. (2013) An everyday activity as a treatment for depression. *Journal of Affective Disorders*, 150, 1148–51.

[19] Burton, C.M., & King, L.A. (2004) The health benefits of writing about intensely positive experiences. *Journal of Research in Personality*, 38, 150–163.

[20] Park, C. L. & Blumberg, C. J. (2002) Disclosing trauma through writing. *Cognitive Therapy and Research*, 26, 597–616.

[21] Smyth, J., Hockemeyer, J. R. & Tulloch, H., (2008) Expressive writing & post-traumatic stress disorder. *British Journal of Health Psychology*, 1, 85–93.

## Resources

**Project Me 101**
https://daretobehappier.wordpress.com/2012/06/25/project-me-day-1101/
**Jane Talbot**
http://www.daretobehappier.com/project-me-18101-move-and-the-way-will-open/
**Dr Kristin Neff**
http://self-compassion.org/test-how-self-compassionate-you-are/
http://self-compassion.org/category/exercises/
**Dare to Be Happier course information**
www.daretobehappier.com/courses

## Picture credits

**ShutterstockPhotoInc.** 10–11 StudioByTheSea; 14 CHAINFOTO24; 18–19 Alexander Sobol; 26–7 MJTH; 31 Theera Disayarat; 32–3 Blazej Lyjak; 36 Olga Lyubkin; 40–1 Elena Kharichkina; 46 ESB Professional; 50–1 Cristina Conti; 54–5 second Studio; 58–9 Monster Ztudio; 62 Teechai; 66–7 Chinnapong; 71 Dilok Klaisataporn; 72–3 icemanphotos; 80–1 BrAt82; 88–9 Cristina Conti; 91 I Water; 94–5 Art Stocker; 98 Izf; 102–3 Masson; 106 Nika Photo; 110–11 frankie's; 116–17 BrAt82; 124–5 Chinnapong; 130–1 AstroStar; 134 eldar nurkovic; 138–9 Izf; 142 2shrimpS; 146–7 chuanpis; 152 Kasetskiy; 156–7 Tonktiti; 161 Pushish Images; 164–5 Izf; 170 Tinnakorn jorruang; 174–5 Bonsales; 178 Roman Samborskyi; 182–3 Song_about_summer; 188 essaya; 192–3 Korawat photo shoot; 195 Onchira Wongsiri; 198–9 KieferPix.